19892

Time Out for Sports

DATE DUE

JUL. 24 1997			

$ 4.95

A *SPORTS ILLUSTRATED* FOR KIDS BOOK

First Edition

Library of Congress Cataloging-in-Publication Data
Cohen, Neil, 1953–
   Jackie Joyner-Kersee/Neil Cohen. — 1st ed.
     p. cm.
   "A sports illustrated for kids book."
   Summary: A biography of the Olympic gold medalist and world champion in both the long jump and the heptathlon.
   ISBN 0-316-15047-9
   1. Joyner-Kersee, Jacqueline, 1962– — Juvenile literature. 2. Women track and field athletes — United States — Biography — Juvenile literature. [1. Joyner-Kersee, Jacqueline, 1962– 2. Track and field athletes. 3. Afro-Americans — Biography.]
I. Title.
GV697.J69C65 1992
796.42'092 — dc20   91-43796

SPORTS ILLUSTRATED FOR KIDS is a trademark of THE TIME INC. MAGAZINE COMPANY

Sports Illustrated For Kids Books is an imprint of Little, Brown and Company.

10 9 8 7 6 5 4 3 2

SEM

For further information regarding this title, write to Little, Brown and Company, 34 Beacon Street, Boston, MA 02108

Published simultaneously in Canada by Little, Brown & Company (Canada) Limited

Printed in the United States of America

Written by Neil Cohen
Cover photograph by Tony Duffy/Allsport USA
Cover design by Pegi Goodman
Comic strip illustrations by Brad Hamann
Produced by Angel Entertainment, Inc.

Contents

1

The World's Greatest Athlete

On the afternoon of September 24, 1988, Jackie Joyner-Kersee paced restlessly back and forth across the red track of Olympic Stadium in Seoul, South Korea. This is it, she thought; this is the race I've been waiting for all my life.

Jackie was getting ready for the start of the 800-meter run, the final event of the heptathlon. The heptathlon is called the most exhausting competition in women's track and field. Over two days, athletes compete in seven events: the 100-meter hurdles, the high jump, the shot put, the 200-meter run, the long jump, the javelin, and the 800 meters. They receive points based on how far they throw, how high they jump, and how fast they run.

After competing in the first six events against the best heptathletes in the world, Jackie was in first place. She was just one event away from winning a gold medal in the Olympics. Jackie was 26 years old. She had been working toward this moment since she first began competing seriously at the age of 14.

As she walked to the starting line for the 800 meters, Jackie thought about how close she had come to capturing the gold medal just four years earlier. In the 1984 Olympics in Los Angeles, Jackie had missed winning the heptathlon by only five points. Five points is a tiny amount in the heptathlon, in which athletes rack up points by the thousands. Jackie had suffered an injury to the hamstring muscle in the back of her left leg and run the 800 meters *one-third of a second* too slow to win the gold. "I always think about 1984," she said later. "So many people gave me so much support after *not* winning. I wanted to give something back."

It was a sunny day in Seoul. High overhead flew banners with the Olympic motto written in Latin: *Citius Altius Fortius*, which means Faster, Higher, Stronger. The crowd quieted in anticipation of the start of the race.

Jackie had proved herself to be the fastest, highest,

strongest so far. But she had to wonder if she could go any farther. A knee injury she had suffered in the previous day's competition had begun to bother her.

Jackie had started out well, winning the 100-meter hurdles race in 12.69 seconds, an Olympic heptathlon best. (Heptathlon records can only be set after all seven events have been completed. High scores for individual events are called bests.) The 100-meter hurdles is a 100-yard sprint, in which the runners must leap over 10 hurdles.

But then disaster struck. In the second event, the high jump, the athlete must leap over a bar suspended so delicately between two upright poles that the slightest touch will topple it. In planting her left foot to make her jump, Jackie badly twisted her knee. She ended up having to settle for a jump of 6'1 1/4", well below her best of 6'4".

One reason the heptathlon is so difficult is that the athletes often have little time between events to rest. With no time to have her knee treated, Jackie had to take her turn in the shot put competition. In the shot put, a woman must put, or heave, a ball that weighs almost nine pounds as far as she can. Jackie gritted her teeth against the pain, and was able to put the shot 15.8 meters — almost as far as her personal best! Then, in the final event of the day, Jackie won the 200-meter race in 22.56 seconds.

At the end of the first day, Jackie was in first place — and just slightly behind world record pace. But she didn't know for how long. The doctors who examined her knee discovered that the injury was a strained tendon, the fibrous material that connects muscle to bone. There is always a chance that a strained tendon can rupture, or tear. Overnight, her physical therapist treated her knee to help reduce the swelling and ease the pain.

Shaky but stable, Jackie came out the next morning for the fifth event of the heptathlon, the long jump. The long jump was Jackie's best event. In the long jump, the athlete sprints down a runway, and then, pushing off a board, leaps as far as she can into a pit full of sand.

In the heptathlon, athletes are permitted three attempts each at the long jump, the high jump, the shot put, and the javelin. Their best effort is the one that counts. Jackie wanted to put all her energy into her first jump, hoping she could pass on the other two jumps and rest her knee. In her only try, she jumped 23'10 1/4" — far enough to set an Olympic heptathlon long-jump record!

The next-to-last event was the javelin. The javelin is a spear-shaped metal pole that measures over seven feet long. After a running start, the athlete attempts to throw the javelin as far as she can.

Jackie wanted to give her best effort, but her injured left leg was the one she always pushed off of when throwing the javelin. And as she pushed off this time, she felt pain in her knee once again. Her best effort was a disappointing 149'10", more than 10 feet shorter than her usual showing.

Going into the final event, Jackie was still in the lead on points. But she had not done as well in the high jump and javelin as she had hoped. And her knee had begun aching again. Jackie remembered how a leg injury had cost her the gold medal in the last Olympics.

At last it was time for the 800-meter run (two laps around the track) to begin. "What do I need?" Jackie asked her coach, Bob Kersee, who is also her husband.

"2:13.67," he said, referring to the time (in minutes, seconds, and hundredths of seconds) in which Jackie needed to run the 800 meters to collect enough points to break the world heptathlon record.

"If I can't run that," she said, "if I can't give the people

5

a world record, I don't deserve to be here."

The starting gun fired and Jackie took off. She wanted to get off to a fast start, perhaps 62 seconds for the first 400 meters. At the end of the first lap, Jackie just trailed the leaders. Natalya Shubenkova [*shoe-beh-COE-va*] of the Soviet Union, who was in the lead, had run the first 400 meters in 62.63 seconds, and Jackie was about a second behind. So far, she was right on schedule.

But then Jackie began to feel some pain, not from her legs, but from her stomach muscles. She remembered how she had held herself back in 1984 because she was worried about her leg, so this time she knew she had to regain her focus quickly. "Block it out, block it out," she told herself. "If your legs aren't burning, you can still run."

Coming around the backstretch, with slightly more than half a lap to go, three East German athletes — Sabine John, Anke Behmer, and Ines Schulz — began to pull away from Jackie. To break the record, she didn't have to *win* the race, but she did have to stay close to the leaders.

Jackie smiled as she crossed the finish line. Although she had finished fifth in the race, she had run it in 2:08.51. Bad knee and all, it was her best time ever. She had scored

987 points, won the gold medal by 293 points over her next competitor, and set a new world record of 7,291 points.

As the Olympic gold medalist and the holder of the world record in the heptathlon, Jackie would also be called "the world's greatest female athlete." The heptathlon was created in 1981 and was first included in the Olympics in 1984. Before that, "the world's greatest female athlete" was the winner of the pentathlon, a five-sport event that included the hurdles, the long jump, the high jump, the shot put, and the 800-meter run. Women competed in the pentathlon from 1927 until 1981, when the 200-meter run and the javelin were added to make a seven-event sport called the heptathlon (*hepta* is the Greek word for seven; *penta* is the Greek word for five).

After her disappointing silver medal finish in the 1984 Olympics, Jackie had streaked like a comet across the track and field sky. Her dominance in the heptathlon, as well as her success in the long jump and the hurdles, was so great that people were starting to call Jackie not just the world's greatest female athlete, but the world's greatest athlete.

"Don't bet that the world's greatest athlete will be in the Super Bowl, the World Series, Centre Court at Wimbledon, or the prize ring at Caesar's Palace," wrote columnist Jim Murray in *The Los Angeles Times*.". . . The world's greatest athlete may very well be just a slip of a girl and not a hunk at all — just 5'10" and 155 — who can cook, has brown eyes and a nice smile, and a figure that could make a chorus line."

Back in Olympic Stadium, the day after her victory, Jackie stood on the highest level of the awards platform, a gold medal around her neck. The crowd stood and the "Star Spangled Banner" trumpeted through the air. Jackie thought about how far she had come.

She had come much farther than the thousands of miles that lie between Seoul and East St. Louis, Illinois, where Jackie was born. She had come up and over a life filled with hurdles. Jackie had come from a poor family, but her parents had taught her to work hard and never stop hoping. She had overcome poverty, the loss of her mother, illness, and countless injuries and disappointments. Her hope, hard work, and talent had taken her to college, to national and world championships, and now to an Olympic gold medal.

Jackie had learned that life is a lot like a race: It's not where you start, but where you finish that counts.

2

The Girl from Piggott Street

Just across the Mississippi River from the city of St. Louis, Missouri, is its smaller, sister city, East St. Louis, Illinois. In the 1940's and 1950's, East St. Louis was a busy, prosperous place. But as the country moved farther west and railroads gave way to airplanes, East St. Louis became a forgotten place. Factories closed up or moved elsewhere. Stores were boarded up. With no jobs to be found, many people moved to other towns. Some turned to crime. Others just tried to hold on, hoping things would get better.

It was into that kind of poor-but-proud home that Jackie Joyner was born on March 3, 1962. Her great-grandmother, Ollie Mae Johnson, had high hopes when she named the new baby after the woman who was then the First Lady of the United States — President John F. Kennedy's wife, Jacqueline. "Someday this little girl is going to be the first lady of something," Mrs. Johnson said.

Jackie was the second of four children born to Alfred and Mary Joyner. Her parents were not much more than children themselves. Mr. Joyner was 14 and Mrs. Joyner was 16 when they married. Mrs. Joyner was pregnant at the time with Jackie's older brother, Alfred Erick. Two years later, Jackie was born. Two sisters, Angela and Debra, were born soon after.

Mr. Joyner had been a promising athlete — a pole vaulter and a hurdler — at Lincoln High School in East St. Louis, but he had had to leave school and find work in order to support his new wife and baby son. He shined shoes, mowed lawns, and did odd jobs. Mrs. Joyner worked as a nurse's assistant at St. Mary's Hospital. Mrs. Johnson, Jackie's great-grandmother, helped out at home.

The Joyner family lived in a small wooden bungalow at 1433 Piggott Street. There was no heat, and during the winters the whole family slept in the kitchen to be near the stove. There wasn't a lot of food to be had; sometimes the family had to make a dinner out of mayonnaise and bread.

Jackie didn't have many clothes. Her mother insisted that she wear the same dress to school two days in a row. She also had only one pair of shoes, which she wore until they almost fell off her feet.

Mr. Joyner stressed to his children that they should never compare themselves to other families. He said that they should all be thankful for what they had and not complain about what they did not have. "We didn't think we were poor," Jackie remembers. "We didn't have a lot, but we knew our mother and father were doing their very best."

As the oldest girl, Jackie was expected to help around the house and set an example for her younger sisters. She helped with the cooking and cleaning. Her father remembers that she hated washing dishes — and it showed. "There was always egg in the forks when she was finished," he said.

When Jackie was 10, her father took a job working for the railroad in Springfield, Illinois, about two hours away. With Mr. Joyner away so much, most of the responsibility for raising the children fell to Mrs. Joyner. Jackie's mother insisted that the children study hard, get good grades, and be polite to people. She also wanted them to understand that a single mistake can destroy all your life's plans.

"My mother was the foundation," Jackie said. "She didn't want us to be like her — not getting what she wanted because she couldn't go to college. She wanted us to find a way out."

Mrs. Joyner felt she had made a mistake by getting pregnant when she was a teenager. She was determined that her children not do the same. One thing she did was to make Jackie come home every night before the streetlights came on. And Jackie was never to hang around talking to boys.

"Both my folks were frightened of boys," said Jackie. "My mother said, with no chance for negotiation, that I was *not* going out with guys until I was 18. So I threw myself into sports and school."

Still, there was also time for fun. Jackie was given the nickname "Joker" by her family because she loved to play practical jokes. Her brother and her sisters were usually the victims of her pranks. And Jackie has always loved to talk.

Jackie enjoyed both sports and school for the same reasons. She loved improving, learning new things, and earning praise.

"In the fifth grade," she remembers, "the teacher explained how to do long division, and I didn't get it, didn't understand. But I came home and worked it out by myself. I was so thrilled that I called my mother. And then at school I got to sit in front of the class. It was great."

Piggott Street is on East St. Louis's South Side, a rough part of town. The Joyner house was across the street from a liquor store and down the block from a pool hall, but it was also around the corner from the community recreation center. The Mary E. Brown Community Center had a library, a swimming pool, and lots of sports and recreation programs for children. It was able to stay open in such a poor community because of government funding.

The recreation center was the place where Jackie, her brother, and their friends went to stay out of trouble. Al had started going there to learn swimming and diving. When Jackie was 9 years old, she went to the recreation center, too.

Jackie was tall for her age and she had long legs. She had always been a fast runner, so she decided to join the track and field team. But she also signed up for lessons in dance and acting. "Dance was my first love," she recalls. "The instructor cared for me a lot, and he felt that one day I would be on Broadway."

Jackie, her sisters, and their friends got together to form a dance group called the Fabulous Dolls. Jackie even became a cheerleader for the recreation center's teams. It was a way to be around boys without getting her mother angry.

One day at the recreation center, Jackie learned that her dance instructor had died. It was sad and shocking news. That's when Jackie turned her attention to track and field.

The track and field program at the recreation center, coached by Nino Fennoy, had a reputation as one of the best city programs in the country. Coach Fennoy had been a star track and field athlete at Lincoln High School himself. After finishing college at Tennessee State University, he returned to coach in East St. Louis.

Coach Fennoy first saw Jackie at a summer sports program when she was 9. What he remembers about Jackie was "just the happiness. She wanted to be doing what we were doing. I can still see her head with the pigtails, the little skinny legs, the knees, and the smile."

Coach Fennoy's program was a citywide track club for elementary and junior high students. They were called the East St. Louis Railers. Jackie was by no means a star right out of the blocks. She was only the fourth or fifth fastest girl in her age group. She started out running the quarter mile (which is roughly the equivalent of 400 meters, or one lap around the track).

In the first big meet she ever attended, Jackie competed in the quarter mile at the Junior Olympics Regionals in Russellville, Arkansas. The Junior Olympics is a national competition held by the American Athletics Union for athletes from ages 9 to 18.

Jackie's track career didn't get off to a fast start. At the regionals, she ran the quarter mile in 70 or 80 seconds and finished dead last. Jackie received a ribbon for participating in the meet, but she wasn't satisfied. "I decided that this was a challenge and that I was going to do my best," she said.

Coach Fennoy remembers something special about Jackie, even when she was just starting out. "She came to practice," he said. "She had respect for adults, and discipline, and an air of enjoyment, like, 'My parents sent me here to have some fun and learn some things.' She wasn't in a hurry, she never complained."

Coach Fennoy was a great admirer of Ed Temple, a legendary track and field coach at Tennessee State University. Coach Temple's greatest pupil was Wilma Rudolph.

Wilma had suffered as a child from polio, a disease that weakens the muscles and sometimes leaves a person unable to walk. She had overcome the disease to become one of the world's great track and field stars, winning gold medals in the 100 meters, the 200 meters, and the 4 x 100-meter relay at the 1960 Olympics. Coach Fennoy was on the lookout for his own Wilma Rudolph, a girl with great ability and determination. He believed that the athletic-but-raw Jackie might be the one.

"With Jackie, it's like she had the gift," he said. "When I'm speaking of gift, it's not just the athletic portion. She had the mental attitude, the spiritual attitude, to weather the ups and downs."

Coach Fennoy expected great things from Jackie. He required her to keep journals on the team's road trips and corrected her grammar and spelling. "Where you're going," he told her, "you'll need to express yourself with more than your legs and arms."

Coach Fennoy remained a believer even as Jackie continued to struggle. She was just learning how to control those long arms and legs and use them to make her faster. Jackie wondered when she would start winning, but she didn't get down on herself or angry at others. "There was no jealousy or animosity," said Coach Fennoy. "She appreciated the accomplishments of others and used that as fuel to become a better person and athlete."

Jackie began learning to play basketball and volleyball at the recreation center. She also continued to practice on the track. Her brother, Al, laughed at that. One day, when Jackie was 10, 12-year-old Al bragged that he could beat her in a race without practicing. Jackie accepted the challenge and began practicing hard every day.

Soon the day of the race came. Many of the kids from the neighborhood, including all of Al's friends, lined up along the racecourse, which was from the mailbox at the corner of their street to the fence in front of their house. It was a distance of about 70 yards. And Jackie won!

"I felt kind of bad," Jackie said. "I was a girl beating a boy, and Al's friends started calling him names. But by beating Al, I let him know that I wasn't a push-around. And he learned to respect me as an athlete."

Jackie and her brother were always close, but through sports they became even closer — even though Jackie began to beat Al in anything in which they competed. Al said that because of her hard work and dedication, Jackie became a role model for him, although she was two years younger. "I didn't have an older brother," he kidded. "I had Jackie."

Despite all the fun they had playing sports, life was sometimes difficult for the Joyner children. Some nights Jackie's father came home drunk and said things he didn't mean. When Jackie was 11, she watched a man get shot on her street. One day the following year, Jackie's grandmother called to say she would be coming to visit. The next day, Jackie learned that while her grandmother was sleeping the night before, the man with whom she lived had come home drunk and shot her to death.

These were sad and upsetting times. "I remember Jackie and me crying together in a back room of the house," Al said, "swearing that someday we were going to make it. Make it out. Make things different."

3

The Pride of East St. Louis

Sometime between the ages of 12 and 13, the tall, awkward girl with the skinny legs, pigtails, and big smile suddenly turned into an athlete. She was growing into her body, and gaining control of those long legs.

"Those were explosive years for her," remembers Coach Fennoy. "It's as if someone pushed a button and said, 'It's your time.'"

Jackie began winning races. She tried new events and succeeded at those, too. After all of her hard work, athletics was finally coming naturally.

One day at the recreation center, a track coach was gathering sand to make a long-jump pit for one of the older girls. Before he finished, Jackie decided to take a leap herself, just for the fun of it. Without any training, Jackie long-jumped 16'9". That would have been considered a good jump by a high school athlete, but Jackie was only 12 years old! The coach couldn't believe it and asked Jackie to do it again. And she did.

Jackie was excited by her new-found ability in the long jump. She loved the combination of running as fast as she could and then flying though the air. She began practicing by long-jumping off the porch of her house. Her brother and sisters would collect sand in a potato chip bag from the community center and carry it home. Then they would use the sand to create a landing pit at one end of the porch.

Coach Fennoy encouraged his kids to become good all-around athletes. Because Jackie could jump and run fast, he suggested she try competing in the pentathlon.

Jackie practiced hard at the pentathlon. She learned to run over hurdles. (In the 80-meter hurdles, the runner has to leap eight hurdles, each 2'6" high.) She learned how to put the shot, which for her age group weighed six pounds. The athlete spins in a small circle to generate enough power to heave the metal ball with one hand by making a pushing motion from the shoulder. In the high jump, she learned how to twist her body to avoid knocking over the bar. In addition, she built up endurance for the 800-meter run.

In 1976, when she was 14, Jackie qualified to compete in the pentathlon at the National Junior Olympics. Jackie and her teammates desperately wanted to go, but their parents didn't have the extra money needed to pay for the car trip to the competition. So the girls held bake sales, cake walks, and sold penny candy to raise the money. Jackie even skipped lunch some days to save her lunch money for the trip.

Not only did Jackie get to compete in the pentathlon at the Junior Olympics, but her combined score for the hurdles, the long jump, the high jump, the shot put, and the 800-meter run was the highest for the 13- to 14-year-old age group. Jackie had won her first national championship!

During that same year, Bruce Jenner won the gold medal in the decathlon at the Summer Olympic Games in Montreal, Canada. The decathlon, like the pentathlon and heptathlon, is a multi-sport event, but for male athletes only. It consists of 10 events: the high jump, the long jump, the 100-meter dash, the 110-meter hurdles, the 400-meter run, the 1,500-meter run, the shot put, the javelin, the discus, and the pole vault. (The discus is an event in which the athlete hurls a two-and-a-half pound object that looks much like a dinner plate as far as he or she can; in the pole vault, the athlete uses a long pole to propel himself or herself over a bar that is raised higher and higher.)

Seeing the 1976 Olympics on television made a big impression on Jackie. She saw how the crowd in Montreal stood and cheered as Bruce finished the final event — the 1500-meter run, which is almost a mile — to set a new Olympic record for points scored in a decathlon. She heard how excited the television commentators were, calling Bruce "the world's greatest athlete." And after the Olympics, she saw how everyone respected and admired Bruce for what he had accomplished.

Jackie decided she wanted that, too. Her father recalls overhearing Jackie and Al talking on the porch one evening, and Jackie confiding to Al, "One day, I'm going to go to the Olympics."

Jackie was also inspired by the achievements of two other Olympic athletes, both women: Wilma Rudolph and Babe Didrikson Zaharias. She learned about Wilma Rudolph from Coach Fennoy. And she found out about Babe from watching a television program.

Babe Didrikson Zaharias was an Olympic track and field champion who excelled at almost any sport she tried. At the 1932 Olympics in Los Angeles, Babe won gold medals in the 80-meter hurdles and the javelin, and a silver medal in the high jump. "Seeing Babe run the hurdles and play baseball, golf, and basketball was something!" Jackie said. "She was a very tough woman, and I admired her toughness."

Jackie understood that it was the dedication of these women that had enabled them to win Olympic gold medals. It was about this time that Jackie began developing what she now calls her "three D's" — desire, dedication, and deter-mination — that would get her to the top of the sports world. "It was a struggle, but I knew that it would take more than my natural talent to succeed," she said.

Jackie dedicated herself to excelling in sports. She was already considered a top athlete, but that didn't satisfy her. She gave up a part-time job selling popcorn in a movie theater. She also gave up cheerleading. When she wasn't practicing her track and field events or studying, Jackie was playing basketball or volleyball.

The next year, when Jackie was 15, she once again went to the National Junior Olympics to compete in the pentathlon. This time, she won her age group by such a wide margin that her name and photograph made it into *Sports Illustrated*'s "Faces in the Crowd" section.

The following fall, Jackie started classes at Lincoln High School as a tenth-grader. Coach Fennoy was also the coach of Lincoln's girls' track and field team; he had helped more than 50 girls win track scholarships so they could attend college. Jackie joined right away. Besides competing in track, she also went out for the school's volleyball and basketball teams.

In her first season, Jackie started at forward on the basketball team. The team was so good that it was favored to win the Illinois state championship that year. Lincoln made it all the way to the sectional semi-finals, which would determine which team went to the state finals. Lincoln ran off to a big lead and was well on its way to defeating Centralia High when a freak accident occurred: The lights in the gym went out!

The Lincoln girls figured they had the game all wrapped up, so they spent the delay sitting around and chatting. The Centralia team, meanwhile, talked over their strategy and did stretching exercises to keep their muscles loose. After the lights were repaired, the Centralia team came charging back. Jackie and her teammates were taken by surprise. Instead of playing as a team, they started making bad shots and playing individual ball. Lincoln lost the game, and a disappointed Jackie and her teammates spent the rest of the year trying to get over it.

Jackie has always remembered that game. She says that it taught her the importance of teamwork, and how every member of a team must help each other if the team is to win.

She also learned what it takes to be a leader. "I learned to ask myself whether I was doing the things that were in my best interest and in the best interest of the team," she said. "And I learned that as a leader I had to be willing to make the same demands on my teammates."

By her senior year in high school, Jackie had become more of a leader. This time, Lincoln won the state finals. Jackie was a great rebounder, a tough defensive player, and a good scorer when the team needed her points. She was so tough, she could even play with the boys. "When I played ball with my little sister, I had to be physically rough to beat her," said her brother, Al, with pride.

Jackie was so determined that her teams be successful that she took it upon herself to make sure her teammates concentrated on business. "Sometimes my teammates would get mad at me or tease me because I confronted them or told the coach if I thought someone was doing something that could stop the team from winning, like hanging out with a boyfriend instead of going to practice," she remembers. "That didn't make me too popular at first, but after a while my teammates respected me for doing it. They knew that it would help us become champions."

Jackie was known among her friends as "a goody girl," as her friend and former teammate Carmen Cannon-Taylor remembers. But she wasn't always Miss Perfect. There was the time that Jackie convinced Carmen to lie about her age at a national track meet so the two friends would not have to compete against each other.

Then there was the time that Carmen convinced Jackie to cut short a training run for a snack. Because the high school had no track, Coach Fennoy would sometimes map out routes around town for the team to take practice runs. One day that route happened to pass right in front of

Carmen's house. When they passed by, Carmen tempted Jackie to take a break with the promise of Jackie's favorite food: ham sandwiches with mayonnaise, lettuce, and pickles. Then they took a shortcut back to school so the coach wouldn't know they had stopped off.

But Jackie couldn't do wrong for long. That night her conscience started to bother her, and she called Carmen to go out and finish the course in the dark. But they didn't just run the part they had missed. Jackie insisted they run the entire course again.

"She was the captain of the team," Carmen said. "It was 'Get your butt up, we're gonna run.' If you do 100 percent, she'll do 120 percent. We were all disciplined, but she was more disciplined."

Jackie also had a lot of confidence in her ability. Carmen remembers when she and Jackie were introduced to the woman who held the record in the women's long jump. Jackie went up to her and said, politely but firmly, "How are you? I'm going to beat your record."

Carmen said, "Jackie, you don't talk to people like that."

And Jackie said, "It's only the truth."

Jackie's mother was proud and happy with her daughter's participation in sports. Mrs. Joyner felt that if her kids ran all day, then they would be too tired to get into trouble at night.

But Mary Joyner still held fast to her rules. One night, when Jackie was 16, she made the mistake of staying out until 11 p.m., playing basketball at the community center. She had lost track of time, and had broken her mother's rule that she had to be home by the time the streetlights came on. Her mother didn't wait for Jackie to come home to punish her. "She ran over with a switch in her hand," Jackie remembers. "She beat me all the way home with that switch."

Older brother Al would sometimes get into fights by upholding their mother's order that guys stay away from his sister. Al was very proud of Jackie; he even kept a scrapbook of newspaper clippings about his sister's accomplishments.

Al was a member of the Lincoln boys' track team. His specialty was the triple jump, an event that requires the jumper to run, then take a hop, a step, and a jump. The distance of the jump is measured from the takeoff board where the jumper takes his first hop to the spot where he lands after he has made his jump.

28

Al was a good triple jumper, but not a great one. And he had never liked to practice. Jackie tried to push Al. She woke him up in the morning, urging him to go out and train. When Al was in his senior year at Lincoln High, Jackie convinced him that if he would only train harder, he would have a chance to win an athletic scholarship to college.

Al took Jackie's advice, and in his last three weeks of high school, he improved his personal best by two and a half feet, to 50'2 1/2". That was good enough to attract the attention of the coach at Tennessee State University, who offered Al a scholarship. Al accepted the scholarship, and a semester later transferred to Arkansas State.

Jackie, meanwhile, kept getting better and better. She was named captain of both the volleyball and basketball teams. In her last two years at Lincoln, the basketball team had a record of 62-2. In her senior year, she averaged 19.6 points per game, and won one game with a shot from 25 feet out in the final second of play. People still talk about that shot. Lincoln High was so good that year that they beat opponents by an average of 52.8 points per game. And they finally won the state championship.

Jackie also led her track team to three state titles. In the spring of her junior year, she long-jumped a state high school record 20'7 1/2". She was named All-State and All-America in both track and basketball. She also added to her honors by winning two more pentathlon championships at the National Junior Olympics as a member of the East St. Louis Railers. That made her national champion for her age group four years in a row!

By the end of her senior year, in 1980, Jackie had become too good for the Junior Olympics. This time, she was asked to try out in the long jump for the real Olympics! Jackie was thrilled. It was very rare for a high school student to be invited to the Olympic Trials and try out for a spot on the United States team.

Jackie went to the Trials, gave it her all, and jumped a personal best of 20'9 3/4", which was good for eighth place. She missed making the team because only the top three finishers qualify.

As it turned out, no Americans would be going to the Olympics anyway. The Games were scheduled to be held in the city of Moscow in the Soviet Union. The Soviets had recently invaded the country of Afghanistan, a move that had angered the United States and other countries that considered this a violation of international law. President Jimmy Carter of the United States decided that the U.S. team would boycott the 1980 Olympics in Moscow as a protest against the invasion.

Jackie was disappointed, but she was only 18. Besides, she was going to college that fall!

Jackie had applied the same drive, determination, and dedication to academics that she did to athletics. She knew she would have to if she wanted to win an athletic scholarship. Jackie had been an honor student at Lincoln High and she graduated in the top 10 percent of her class.

Jackie was heavily recruited by colleges that offered her scholarships if she would play for their women's basketball teams. Coach Billie Moore of the University of California at Los Angeles (UCLA), which has one of the top teams in the country, thought so highly of Jackie that she traveled to East St. Louis four times to try to talk her into coming to UCLA. Finally, Jackie accepted.

In the fall of 1980, Jackie's dad escorted her to Los Angeles to begin her college career. Jackie had finally made it out of East St. Louis, but she would soon be back.

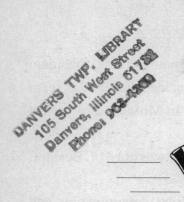

4

On Her Own

Los Angeles, California, with its beaches, palm trees, mansions, and movie stars, is a long way from the south side of East St. Louis, Illinois. For 18-year-old Jackie, it was an exciting place to be.

Jackie was happy finally to be free of her mother's strict rules. But she was not the kind of person to run wild. Besides, she had many things to keep her busy.

When she had accepted the basketball scholarship to UCLA, Jackie had asked for and received Coach Billie Moore's permission to compete also for the women's track and field team — as long as track meets and practices didn't interfere with basketball games and drills. Although her basketball skills were helping to pay for her education, Jackie still dreamed of winning a track and field gold medal at the Olympic Games. "Track has always been my first love," Jackie said. She hoped that the coaching at UCLA and the challenge of competing against the country's best college track stars would help her reach that goal.

Jackie did her best to keep one sport from interfering with the other, and to keep both from getting in the way of the classroom, where she was majoring in history. "I was dedicated to the sport I was playing," she said. "During basketball season, I just worried about basketball and my studies. The same during track season. That discipline helped tremendously."

Jackie's basketball career at UCLA got off to a great start. Basketball practice began in October, and Jackie quickly showed Coach Moore how right she was to have recruited her. Even as a freshman, Jackie was good enough to win a spot on the team as a starter.

Playing at the forward position, Jackie was a team player who didn't need to have the ball to help the UCLA women's basketball team, called the Bruins, win. She was a ferocious rebounder and a hard-nosed defensive player.

"All the old-fashioned words apply to Jackie," says Coach Moore. "Dedication, discipline, hard work."

Jackie's track and field career in college, however, had a bumpier beginning. Jackie wanted to concentrate on the long jump, her favorite event, but because she was not attending UCLA on a track and field scholarship, the coaches regarded her as a walk-on. A walk-on is a student who just happens to walk on to the field and make the team. In college sports, walk-ons are not considered serious athletes the way scholarship players are, and usually do not receive as much attention from the coaches.

When Jackie came over to the track to practice, none of the coaches had much time for her. She would get only bits and pieces of advice. Sometimes one coach would advise her to do the exact opposite from what another coach had just told her.

In East St. Louis, Jackie had had only one coach. Now she had so many different coaches, it was as if she had no coach at all. Jackie was confused, but she was too shy and polite to complain. Instead, she spent a lot of time practicing by herself, jumping over and over again. But her jumping didn't get any better; in fact, it got worse. Even though she had jumped 20'9 3/4" at the Olympic Trials, she found she wasn't able to go much farther than 19 feet.

One of the coaches, Bob Kersee, noticed Jackie's problems. Bob was the new assistant coach in charge of the women sprinters and hurdlers.

Even though he wasn't responsible for the long jumpers, Bob could see that Jackie wasn't getting the right kind of attention. Bob watched Jackie practice and it was obvious to him that she had the running speed and leaping power in her legs to be a great long jumper. All she needed were some lessons in the proper technique. "I saw this talent walking around the campus that everyone was blind to," he said. "No one was listening to her mild requests to do more."

When Christmas arrived, Jackie decided to remain at school and spend the holiday with new friends instead of returning to East St. Louis to spend it with family. It was her first Christmas since leaving for school, and her mother pleaded with her to come home, but Jackie felt she was "too independent now."

Unhappily, Jackie had to go home right after Christmas. In January of 1981, she received a call that her mother had been stricken with a disease called meningitis [*men-in-*

JY-tis]. Meningitis attacks the brain and spinal cord. Jackie's brother, Al, also returned home, coming from Arkansas State, where he was a junior.

By the time Jackie and Al joined their father, two sisters, and their aunt, Della Gaines, at their mother's bedside, Mrs. Joyner had fallen into a coma. A coma is a state of unconsciousness that sometimes happens to very sick people. Mrs. Joyner needed life-support machines to keep her alive. The doctors told the family that they could keep Mrs. Joyner's body alive with the machines, but that the disease had destroyed her brain. She would never wake up from the coma.

Mrs. Joyner had been an active and lively person, and had once said she wouldn't want to be kept alive by machines. But Mr. Joyner couldn't bring himself to make the decision to turn off the life-support system. It was left to the two oldest children, Al and Jackie. But Jackie knew what had to be done. "If we left her on the machines," Jackie said, "she'd never have known us, and she would have continued suffering indefinitely."

The family prayed, and then told the doctors to remove the life-support system. Shortly afterward, Mary Joyner died. She was only 38 years old.

The family was stricken with grief. Mrs. Joyner had been the glue that held them all together through the tough times. At the funeral, one of Jackie's sisters fainted. Jackie felt that she had to be the strong one. "With her gone," Jackie said, "some of her determination passed to me."

Aunt Della took charge of the two younger girls so that Jackie could return to college. Jackie missed her mother deeply. But she felt that being strong meant not expressing her sadness. Instead, she held it inside of her, which made it difficult for her to get past it and get on with her life. Bob Kersee went looking for her to offer his sympathy. Bob, who was 27 at the time, had also lost his mother when he was 18. "I found it amazing because I didn't know him beyond his being a coach," Jackie remembers. "But he said if I had doubts and needed to talk them out, I could come to him."

In the short time he had been at UCLA, Bob had gained a reputation as a tough coach who didn't go in for small talk. But he was genuinely concerned about Jackie. He worried that, as the oldest daughter, Jackie might feel she should quit school to care for the rest of the family. "I tried to protect Jackie from the 'Now I'm the mom' syndrome," Bob recalls.

Bob also wanted to help Jackie get her track and field career out of the rut in which it had gotten stuck. Bob thought, as Nino Fennoy had when Jackie was a kid, that Jackie had too much talent to tie it all up in one event. He had heard how well Jackie had performed in the pentathlon at the National Junior Olympics. Now a new event was being added to track competitions that seemed made for Jackie: the heptathlon.

UCLA didn't have an assistant coach for the women's multi-events. Bob decided to talk to the women's athletic director, Dr. Judith Holland, about letting him take on the added responsibility of coaching Jackie.

It was unusual to have one coach work with one athlete in different areas, but Bob felt that Jackie was an unusual athlete. Bob believed so strongly in Jackie's ability that he remembered putting it to Dr. Holland as more of an ultimatum than a request. "Either I coached her in the hurdles, long jump, and multi-events, or I'd quit," he said, "because to go on as she had would be an abuse of her talent."

Dr. Holland asked Jackie if this was what she wanted to do. Competing in the heptathlon was not something Jackie had always dreamed of, but she was willing to give it a try.

"I went along because the heptathlon was less boring than jumping," Jackie said later. "I used to hate waiting around for the meet to end after my one little event was over." Besides, she thought, Coach Fennoy had been right about the pentathlon, and Bob was very excited about her possibilities in the heptathlon. The heptathlon would be an Olympic sport in 1984. Maybe this new sport would be her ticket to the Games.

But first there would be a lot of hard work ahead. Training for the heptathlon meant training for seven different events, at some of which Jackie had never done very well. She could run sprints, hurdle, long-jump, and high-jump, but she had never had much success at the shot put and the 800-meter run. The javelin? Well, the first time Jackie tried to throw one, she hit herself in the head with it.

"I enjoyed doing different events and not trying to single one out," Jackie recalls. "But I needed to work on all my events, especially the technical events." By the technical events, Jackie meant the shot put and the javelin. Jackie had put the shot in the pentathlon, but now it weighed 8 pounds 13 ounces instead of 6 pounds. The javelin also made her feel clumsy. It weighs 1 pound 10 ounces and is more than

7 feet long. Throwing one requires the athlete to run side-ways, performing a series of cross-over steps, before launch-ing it into the air.

Training for all of these events meant sacrificing time from basketball and her favorite track event, the long jump. Jackie complained about that to Bob. Sometimes she got frustrated that all the training time was not producing fast results. She and Bob would argue. Bob tried to convince Jackie that she had the potential to be the world champion and set new records. Then Jackie would go back to work.

It wasn't easy to measure Jackie's progress in the heptathlon. As with the other multi-event sports, the heptathlon is scored in a very complicated way. Each athlete's time in a race, height or distance in a jump, and distance in a throw is worth a certain number of points according to a special heptathlon table. The table awards many points for an extraordinary performance, fewer for an average job, and so on down the line.

The points that an athlete collects at each event are added up to determine her total score. An athlete who has difficulty with one or two events can still do well if she can dominate two or three of the other events. The heptathlete with the highest total score wins the competition.

Each competition divides the events over two days. The 100-meter hurdles, high jump, shot put, and 200-meter sprint are held on the first day; the long jump, javelin, and 800-meter run on the second. Because it is such an exhausting sport, college athletes generally compete in only one or two heptathlons each year.

In the spring of her freshman year, Jackie competed in her first heptathlon at the Association of Intercollegiate Athletics for Women national championships in Tacoma, Washington. She wasn't expecting to do very well, and after the first day of competition, Jackie was far behind the leaders.

But Jackie would soon learn the power of good coaching. That night, back in the motel where they were staying, Bob prepared Jackie for the first event of the second day's competition: the long jump. He used masking tape to turn the motel hallway into a long-jump runway and worked with Jackie on her approach and takeoff.

The next morning, Jackie long-jumped 21 feet in competition. It was her best jump since high school. In one evening, Bob had helped Jackie improve in her *best* event.

Jackie finished strongly in the second day's events and racked up enough points to finish in third place.

Jackie had already come so far so fast that Bob began to sense Jackie's future greatness in the sport. "I could see she'd be the world record holder," he recalls.

One day during her sophomore year, Bob sat down with Jackie. He compared her score in each of the events with winning scores to show Jackie where she needed work. "Bob showed me on paper first," Jackie says. "Jane Frederick [the best American heptathlete] was beating me by 400 points in just two events, the shot put and the javelin." What's more, although Jackie had great speed, she lost in the hurdles. Bob worked with her to develop the proper technique to make the best use of her speed and the spring in her legs.

To help fine-tune her training program, Bob brought Jackie to see Bob Forster, a highly regarded Los Angeles physical therapist, for an evaluation. "She was like a gem in the raw," Bob Forster remembers. "After examining her, though, I told him: 'This girl's the real thing.'"

Things seemed to be going so well for Jackie. But then life threw another hurdle in her path. During her workouts that spring, Jackie often had to stop suddenly. She would double over and gasp for breath. She felt as if she couldn't breathe. It was a frightening experience.

After a few of these episodes, Jackie went to a doctor and learned that she was suffering from asthma. Asthma is an illness in which the breathing tubes tighten up, making it difficult for a person to breathe. It can be caused by many things, including allergies, stress, and air pollution. In Jackie's case, the doctors believed the asthma was caused by exercise. Jackie wasn't about to give up her athletic career when it was just getting started. She took medication as she needed it, and rested when an attack came on.

Although the asthma interfered with Jackie's training, it was during her sophomore year that she began to show the kind of greatness that Bob had predicted for her. Jackie was able to win the two major heptathlons of the summer: the National Collegiate Athletic Association championship as the top collegiate heptathlete, and the national championship, conducted by The Athletics Congress, the governing body of track and field in the United States, as the best heptathlete in the country. Jackie's 6,099 score in the college championships was an NCAA record. For her performance on the basketball court and on the track, she was named

UCLA's All-University Athlete.

Jackie kept up the pace into her junior year, too. During basketball season, Jackie averaged 8.8 points and 5.6 rebounds and was named most valuable player on the team. That June, Jackie again won the NCAA championship in the heptathlon with a record-setting score (6,365 points), and was named MVP of the UCLA women's track team, too. Jackie had had a double MVP year and was named All-University Athlete for the second time. She was also honored with the Broderick Award as the nation's top collegiate track performer.

Late in the summer of 1983, Jackie and her brother, Al, shared a thrill when they both made the U.S. team that would compete in the world championships of track and field in Helsinki, Finland. It would be their first time competing for a world championship.

Jackie and Al had become even closer in the years since their mother's death. They spoke often on the phone, and sometimes appeared at the same track meets. Brother and sister seemed to do especially well at meets that they both attended. "We've got a special kind of ESP," Al says.

Both hoped to do well in Helsinki, but their hopes were

quickly dashed. Al suffered a hamstring pull during the triple jump competition. Jumpers in the open competition get six tries at their event, and their best effort is the one that counts. Slowed by his injury, Al's best jump was good for only eighth place.

Jackie, meanwhile, neglected to take proper care of herself between days of the heptathlon competition. Her usual routine was to apply ice to her sore legs after the first day in order to keep her muscles from getting sore. But this time, she didn't. She woke up the next morning with her legs aching, and during warm-ups, she pulled a hamstring muscle, too. Hobbled by the injury, Jackie had to withdraw from the competition.

Both Jackie and Al were disappointed. Neither one had been able to show the world what he or she could really do. But they had come too far — together and separately — to become discouraged now.

"Jackie," Al said to his sister in Helsinki, "it's just not our time yet."

5

Silver Medal, Diamond Ring

The city of Los Angeles was buzzing at the start of 1984. It was an Olympic year, and the city was going to host the Summer Games. It would be the first time since 1932 that the Summer Olympics would be held in the United States; that year they were held in Los Angeles, too.

Jackie had looked forward to competing in the Olympic Games since she had watched them on television in 1976 when Bruce Jenner won the decathlon. To help Jackie concentrate all of her energy on preparing for the Olympics, Bob convinced her to sit out the 1983-84 basketball and track seasons. Under NCAA rules, college athletes are allowed to miss one year without losing their scholarships. They are eligible to compete in their sports for four years, but they have five years in which to do it. Jackie decided she would give up the year now, and stay on at UCLA for a fifth year.

Basketball coach Billie Moore had no objection; she was happy to help Jackie realize her dream. "If I coached another 40 years, I don't think I could find someone else like Jackie," she said. "She's a winner and a competitor. She knows how to prepare and what it takes to win. . . . But as great an athlete as she is, she's an even greater human being."

With no basketball practice to worry about, Jackie did just two things. She went to class and she went to the track to practice her long jump and heptathlon events.

Track and field has an indoor season in winter and an outdoor season in the spring and summer. For the indoor season, Jackie would usually train for and compete in the sprints, hurdles, and long jump; there is no indoor heptathlon competition. She would also bundle up, by Southern California standards, and go outside to practice her technique in the javelin and shot put, too. She put in eight hours of training each day.

"It takes a lot of time, a lot of juggling, a lot of organization, and a lot of detail work trying to figure out which event to work on first, what each event should be focused on," explained Bob. "And we just work day by day, week by week, trying to get all these little things down."

Often, Jackie's brother, Al, would also be training just across the track at UCLA's Drake Stadium. Al had completed his college eligibility, but he was still competing nationally and internationally in the triple jump. He had seen how much Jackie had improved while working with Bob, and thought that perhaps Bob would be able to help him improve, too. With Jackie's encouragement, Al moved to Los Angeles to train with Bob.

Al was a fast runner, but he had trouble taking his speed coming down the runway and turning it into distance in his jump. Bob worked with Al on improving his body control as he went into his hop, step, and jump. The UCLA assistant coach was beginning to build a reputation as one of the brightest young track and field coaches in the country.

Being a coach was something Bob had always wanted to be. He had been a good athlete, but he was never world class. And he has always loved studying what makes things tick. "Even as a kid, I studied track from a coach's point of view," he said.

Bob was born in Panama, a small country in Central America best known as the site of the Panama Canal. His mother was Panamanian and his father was an American stationed in Panama with the U.S. Navy. Because of his father's career with the Navy, Bob spent his childhood moving from state to state, wherever his father was stationed. Finally, he ended up in California.

Bob's idol growing up was Vince Lombardi, the legendary football coach. "I dreamed of being the first NFL black coach, then the Olympic coach, and finally I cut that down and started coaching Olympic athletes," Bob said.

After graduating from Long Beach State in 1976, with a degree in exercise physiology, Bob was studying for his master's degree at Cal State-Northridge, when he left to take the job as assistant track coach at UCLA.

Bob kept an office in Drake Stadium, where his desk was two hurdles covered with a piece of plywood. But his classroom was the track. He understood track and field events well enough to break down an athlete's performance to the smallest movements and make corrections when necessary.

Bob would try to inspire his athletes to win by telling

them how good they could be. He had a bit of the preacher in him; his grandfather had been a Baptist minister, and Bob himself was associate pastor of St. Luke's Baptist Church, near his home in Long Beach.

But Bob could also be as demanding as a marine drill sergeant when it came to workouts. Once, he had Jackie train by running up and down the hundreds of steps that go from the field to the top of Drake Stadium. When Jackie complained, he reminded her of her Olympic goal. "Do you want to win the gold medal or the silver medal?" he asked her. "Do you want to be standing there listening to the East German national anthem?" Silenced, Jackie ran back up the steps.

Jackie started off her competitive year on a high note. In January, she traveled to Chicago, Illinois, to compete in the long jump at the Bally Invitational meet. Jackie always enjoyed competing in the long jump, and the indoor season gave her a chance to concentrate more on it. "Jumping has always been the thing to me," she once explained. "It's like leaping for joy, but of course there's more to it than that. Your competitor has just done 21 feet, another competitor is on the runway, and I'm behind her. You have to respond here and now. It lets you know what you're made of."

In Chicago, Jackie showed the country what she was made of. She long-jumped 21'6 3/4" to set a new American indoor record. The old record of 21'6 1/2" was held by Carol Lewis. Carol was a long jumper at the University of Houston and the sister of Carl Lewis, the great sprinter and long jumper.

Back at home, Jackie continued her eight-hour-a-day training schedule for the Olympics. As much as she didn't particularly enjoy training for the javelin and shot put, she concentrated her efforts on those two because they were her weakest events. She lifted weights to build up her arms and upper-body strength. She spent hours perfecting her technique, practicing the run-up for the javelin and the power-generating spin for putting the shot. She hoped all of her hard work would pay off at the Olympic Trials in June.

In order for an athlete to make the U.S. Olympic team, he or she must compete with the other great American athletes in their sport at the Olympic Trials. It is a national championship track meet, in which the top three finishers in each event qualify to become members of the Olympic team. The Trials in 1984 were going to be held at the site of the

Olympic Games — in Los Angeles.

Jackie expected her toughest competition to come from Jane Frederick. Jane was 32, 10 years older than Jackie. In the United States, she had dominated the heptathlon, and before that the pentathlon, for 10 years. Jane held the American record of 6,457 points. The 1984 Games would be the first — and at her age, probably the last — time she would have the chance to compete in an Olympic heptathlon. Jane was determined to make the team. So were Jodi Anderson, from Chicago, the 1980 heptathlon trials winner; Cindy Greiner, an experienced heptathlete from Eugene, Oregon; and Patsy Walker, another practiced heptathlete, who had also attended UCLA and then the University of Houston.

So the best heptathletes in the country gathered in Los Angeles, all vying for the three spots on the team. Jackie started out well on the first day, winning her heat in the first event, the 100-meter hurdles, in a time of 13.61 seconds. But then Jodi Anderson took the point lead when she ran a 13.52 in the next heat.

The field stayed tight through the shot put, which was won by Patsy Walker with a toss of 46'3/4". But all the athletes received a shock at the high jump. Jane Frederick, who had been suffering from a leg injury, was unable to make the minimum height of 5'7 1/4" that high jumpers are required to clear to continue in the competition.

Jackie was shocked and sorry for Jane. But she pulled herself together and was able to clear 6 feet. Jodi Anderson jumped 5'10 3/4". Jackie then pulled into a 15-point lead.

Jackie increased her lead in the 200-meters, finishing with a time of 23.77 seconds. Cindy turned in a time of 24.46, Jodi a 24.49, and Patsy a 24.68. After the first day, Jackie was in first place, but the top four were so close together in points that anything could happen.

The next morning, the heptathletes began the second day's competition with the long jump. Cindy long-jumped 19'9 3/4". Patsy leaped 20'4 1/2", a personal best. Then Jodi, who, like Jackie, is a world class long jumper, soared 20'10 1/2". But Jackie blew them all away. Jackie came galloping down the runway, sailed through the air, and stretched for every inch to hit 22'4 1/4". It was a new American heptathlon long-jump best, breaking Jodi's mark of 21'9 1/2". Jackie had jumped a foot and a half farther than her nearest competitor had. All of a sudden, it became clear that Jackie was on pace to break Jane Frederick's American heptathlon record of 6,458 points.

There were just two events left, the javelin and the 800 meters, neither Jackie's strengths. But during the lunch break, Jane Frederick came over to talk to her. In a fine display of sportsmanship, Jane encouraged Jackie to break her record. "Go for it," she said.

In the javelin, all four women threw for personal bests. Patsy threw 130'9", Cindy 138'8", Jackie 148'11", and Jodi a colossal 159'2".

Jackie went into the final event, the 800 meters, still ahead on points, and needing a time of 2:18.1 to set the record. She did better than that. Although Patsy Walker won the race in 2:12.57, Jackie finished close behind. Her 2:13.41 gave her enough points to win the heptathlon and to set a new American record of 6,520 points. Jodi Anderson (6,413) was just 107 points behind and finished second, and Cindy Greiner (6,204) was third. The trio would represent the U.S. at the Olympics.

It was the best heptathlon of Jackie's career. Her smile got even bigger when she learned that Al had also qualified for the U.S. Olympic team in the triple jump with the third best jump of the competition. A few days later, Jackie also qualified to represent her country in the open long-jump competition. She was going to the Olympics, at last, with not one, but two chances for a gold medal!

Then, with two weeks to go before the start of the Olympics, bad luck hit. In the middle of a training session, Jackie strained her left hamstring muscle. Fortunately, it was not serious enough to keep her out of the Games, but it did cut down her training time. She needed physical therapy and a lot of rest.

In August, the Olympics arrived in Los Angeles. The whole country was fired up. The United States had boycotted the 1980 Summer Olympics in Moscow, and Americans were eager to root for their athletes against the rest of the world's.

Unfortunately, some of the best athletes from the rest of the world were sitting this one out themselves. The Soviet Union and its allies, including East Germany and Cuba, had decided to boycott the Olympics in retaliation for the U.S. boycott of the Moscow Games in 1980.

The athletes from the country that was East Germany until 1990 were considered to be the best heptathletes in the world. With Jane Frederick and the East Germans staying at home, the media tabbed Jackie as the odds-on favorite to win the gold medal in the event. Jackie, however, was worried about her left hamstring. She was also concerned about Jodi Anderson and two other strong heptathletes on the international circuit, Judy Simpson of Great Britain and Glynis Nunn of Australia.

Jackie had never competed against Glynis before. She didn't know how good she was, but the reports were impressive. "I kept seeing her name in the paper," Jackie recalled. "Bob told me not to worry about her, just to do the best I could and that would be enough. But I couldn't stop thinking about her."

Jackie went into the competition with her leg heavily bandaged. After the first day, through the 100-meter hurdles, the shot put, the high jump, and the 200-meter run, Jackie was in second place with 3,739 points, just behind Judy Simpson, who had 3,759, and just ahead of Glynis Nunn, who had 3,731.

On the second day, Jackie hoped to do particularly well in the long jump, her best event, and take a big lead. In the heptathlon, competitors get three tries at each of the jumping and throwing events. The best jump or throw each competitor makes is the one that counts in the scoring.

With Jackie's stride thrown off by her injury, she fouled in her first two tries at the long jump, then had to move cautiously in her third. (A long-jump foul occurs when the jumper pushes off past the takeoff board.) Jackie jumped only 20'1/2", more than two feet shorter than she had leaped at the Trials. She took the lead, but only barely, as Judy slipped back.

Going into the final event, the 800 meters, Jackie was still in first place, but she held a mere 31-point lead over Glynis. What's more, she was tired and hurting. But Bob figured out that if Jackie could stay close to Glynis and finish only 2.13 seconds behind her, a distance of about 14 yards, she could still win the gold medal.

At the same time, just across the track, the triple-jump competition was going on. In the open jumping and throwing competitions, competitors get six attempts, with their best jump or throw counting. Al Joyner was only the third best jumper on the American team; he wasn't given much of a chance. But after three rounds, Al was in the lead with a jump of 56'7 1/2", his personal best by nearly three inches.

As the fourth round of jumping began, Al looked across

the track and saw Jackie lining up for the 800 meters. Al passed on his fourth jump and ran across the infield to the edge of the final turn of the race.

In the 800 meters, the runners have to run twice around the track oval. The first time, Glynis was in front. Al shouted to Jackie to stay close. The second time, with 150 yards to go, Glynis led Jackie by almost 20 yards. Al went wild. He started running alongside his sister on the infield grass. "Pump your arms, Jackie!" he screamed. "This is it!"

Glynis crossed the finish line in 2:10.57. Jackie followed in 2:13.03, a third of a second too slow. She had lost the gold medal to Glynis by only five points: 6,390 to 6,385.

Al went back to the triple-jump competition to wait while his competitors tried to beat his jump. When no one could, he became the first American in 80 years to win a gold medal in the triple jump. Then he went over to the awards stand. Jackie had just stepped off the platform with a silver medal around her neck. She was crying.

Al put his arms around his sister to give her a hug. "It's okay," he said. "It's okay."

But Jackie's tears were not tears of disappointment, but were tears of joy. "I'm not crying because I lost," she said.

"I'm crying because you won. You fooled them all."

A few days later, Jackie was scheduled to compete in the open long-jump competition. Once again, her leg injury prevented Jackie from going all out. She finished a disappointing fifth.

Still, it had been a very successful Olympics for the whole hometown crew from UCLA. Seven of the athletes who Bob coached — including Al and sprinter Valerie Brisco — had won gold medals in individual events or relays. Another, Florence Griffith, had won the silver medal in the 200-meter dash.

And Jackie and Al had made history by becoming the first brother and sister to win Olympic medals in track and field on the same day. Months later, when Al returned to East St. Louis, he said people would stop him on the street, but not because of his gold medal performance in the triple jump. "You're the guy who cheered for his sister," they would say.

Jackie refused to blame her failure on her injury; she did not want to say anything to diminish Glynis's victory. She felt she had let herself get psyched out by reading Glynis's newspaper clippings. "I learned to focus on what

Jackie Joyner is doing," Jackie said. "Not to underestimate others, but just get the job done and let the others come after her."

Soon after the Olympics, at a meet in France, Jane Frederick charged back into action, and took back the American heptathlon record with a score of 6,803 points. But Jane knew her days as U.S. record holder were numbered; Jackie was coming on.

"I always thought she would be the one to lead the next generation, and it had to do with the kind of person she was," Jane said. "She had a sense of purpose. With Kersee's direction, she really gave herself to all seven events."

Jackie's Olympic setback inspired her to work even harder when she returned to UCLA for classes in the fall of 1984. She was eager to return to the basketball team. "I enjoy playing basketball and I miss it," she once said.

In her final season, Jackie scored an average of 12.7 points per game and was the team's top rebounder with 9.3 rebounds per game. She led the Bruins to a 20-10 record and was named first-team All-Conference.

Jackie finished her basketball career as the school's fourth leading career rebounder and sixth best career scorer.

Jackie and Al Joyner, along with their two sisters, grew up in this house in East St. Louis, Illinois. A basketball scholarship took Jackie to UCLA, where she was twice named Most Valuable Player in the sport.

Jackie's UCLA Basketball Career

Year	G	FG%	FT%	REB	AVG	A	TP	AVG
1980-81	34	.506	.633	158	4.6	78	314	9.2
1981-82	30	.381	.677	174	5.8	69	239	8.0
1982-83	28	.414	.657	156	5.6	51	246	8.8
1983-84				(Did not play)				
1984-85	29	.464	.459	264	9.1	41	368	12.7
Total	121	.446	.585	752	6.2	239	1167	9.6

Jackie shared scrapbooks and some laughs with her brother, Al, her younger sister, Angela, and her Aunt Della (far left). Growing up, Jackie liked to play practical jokes. It's no wonder that they nicknamed her "Joker."

U.S. Women's Long Jump Records

Jackie Joyner-Kersee	Pan Am Games	1987	24' 5 1/2"
Jackie Joyner-Kersee	San Diego	1988	24' 3"
Jackie Joyner-Kersee	World Champ.	1987	24' 1 3/4"
Jackie Joyner-Kersee	Pan Am Games	1987	23' 9 1/2"
Jackie Joyner-Kersee	Zurich	1985	23' 9"
Jackie Joyner-Kersee	Olympic Trials	1988	23' 8 1/4"
Jackie Joyner-Kersee	Pan Am Games	1987	23' 8"
Jackie Joyner-Kersee	Pan Am Games	1987	23' 5 1/2"
Jackie Joyner-Kersee	Pan Am Games	1987	23' 4 3/4"
Jackie Joyner-Kersee	Brussels	1986	23' 4 1/2"

In 1987, Jackie won the 55-meter hurdles at the Vitalis/U.S. Olympic Invitational meet at the Meadowlands in East Rutherford, New Jersey. Her time was 7:45, a meet record. She also won the long jump with a leap of 21' 10", another meet record. She was named the meet's outstanding athlete.

At the 1986 Goodwill Games in Moscow, Jackie, shown long-jumping, not only broke the world record in the heptathlon, but was the first woman to score 7,000 points in that event.

Jackie received the Sullivan Award, given by the Amateur Athletics Union, in 1986. She beat out U.S. Naval Academy basketball star David Robinson and University of Miami quarterback Vinny Testaverde for the honor.

Jackie gives her husband and coach, Bob Kersee, a workout on the track. Jackie herself usually trains five days a week for five hours each day. When training for the Olympics, she worked out eight hours a day.

At the 1988 Olympic Trials in Indianapolis, Jackie set an American heptathlon best in the 200-meter sprint. She also set two other American bests, in the 100-meter hurdles and the high jump. Her score of 7,215 broke her own world record in the heptathlon. She also set a mark for the first day of competition with a score of 4,367. Jackie finished an astonishing 989 points ahead of the the second-place finisher, despite temperatures over 100 degrees.

Jackie set an American heptathlon best in the high jump at the 1988 Olympic Trials in Indianapolis, Indiana.

Jackie's Heptathlon Bests

100-Meter Hurdles	Olympic Games	1988	12.69
High Jump	Olympic Trials	1988	6' 4"*
Shot Put	World Champ.	1987	52' 6"
200 Meters	Olympic Trials	1988	22.30**
Long Jump	Olympic Games	1988	23' 10 1/4"**
Javelin	Olympic Festival	1986	164' 5"
800 Meters	US-USSR Meet	1982	2:09.32

* American Best
** World Best

*The shot put has never been easy for Jackie,
but she always gets "A" for effort.*

Heptathlon World Bests

100-Meter Hurdles	Sabine Paetz	GDR	1984	12.64
High Jump	Chris Stanton	AUS	1985	6' 5"
Shot Put	Eva Wilms	GFR	1979	68' 8 1/2"
200 Meters	Joyner-Kersee	USA	1988	22.30
Long Jump	Joyner-Kersee	USA	1988	23' 10 1/4"
Javelin	Tessa Sanderson	UK	1981	212' 1"
800 Meters	Nadine Debois	FR	1987	2:01.84

Tony Duffy/Allsport USA

Jackie gets set for the javelin on the second day of the heptathlon at the '88 Olympics in Seoul. She was leading, in spite of a twisted knee suffered on the first day.

After winning a silver medal in the heptathlon at the '84 Olympics, Jackie was determined to get the gold in '88 — and she did!

All-Time Heptathlon Leaders

Jackie Joyner-Kersee	USA	Olympic Games	1988	7,291
Jackie Joyner-Kersee	USA	Olympic Trials	1988	7,215
Jackie Joyner-Kersee	USA	Olympic Festival	1986	7,158
Jackie Joyner-Kersee	USA	Goodwill Games	1986	7,148
Jackie Joyner-Kersee	USA	World Champ.	1987	7,128
Larissa Nikitina	USSR	Bryansk	1989	7,007
Jackie Joyner-Kersee	USA	San Jose	1987	6,979
Sabine Paetz	GDR	Potsdam	1984	6,946
Ramona Neubert	GDR	Moscow	1983	6,935
Jackie Joyner-Kersee	USA	Mt. SAC Relays	1986	6,910

Jackie and her sister-in-law, Florence Grif-fith-Joyner, sport their gold medals at the 1988 Olympics. Jackie won the gold in the long jump and in the heptathlon, while Flo-Jo won gold medals in the 100 meters, 200 meters, and as a member of the 4 x 100 relay team.

IT IS HARD TO BELIEVE, BUT OLYMPIC HEPTATHLETE JACKIE JOYNER-KERSEE ALMOST DID NOT GET TO COMPETE IN TRACK AND FIELD AT ALL.

BECAUSE JACKIE WAS ATTENDING UCLA ON A BASKETBALL SCHOLARSHIP, THE TRACK AND FIELD COACHES PAID LITTLE ATTENTION TO HER. BUT JACKIE KEPT PRACTICING, WHICH DID NOT GO UN-NOTICED BY TOUGH ASSISTANT COACH, BOB KERSEE.

I WONDER WHO THAT GIRL IS.

BOB DECIDED TO TALK TO DR. JUDY HOLLAND, THE UCLA WOMEN'S ATHLETIC DIRECTOR, ABOUT LETTING HIM COACH JACKIE.

SHE'S NOT HERE ON A TRACK AND FIELD SCHOLARSHIP. JACKIE'S HERE ON A BASKETBALL SCHOLARSHIP.

ALL THAT TALENT GOING TO WASTE. EITHER I COACH HER IN THE HURDLES, LONG JUMP, AND MULTI-EVENTS, OR I QUIT!

WELL, I'M WILLING TO GIVE IT A TRY. BUT THE FINAL DECISION IS JACKIE'S!

IN THE SPRING OF HER FRESHMAN YEAR, JACKIE QUALIFIED FOR THE NCAA HEPTATHLON CHAMPIONSHIPS. AFTER THE FIRST DAY OF COMPETITION, BOB USED MASKING TAPE TO TURN THE MOTEL HALLWAY INTO A LONG JUMP RUNWAY. THE NEXT DAY, JACKIE JUMPED WELL ENOUGH TO FINISH THIRD IN THE HEPTATHLON.

I THINK I FOUND YOUR PROBLEM. LET'S WORK ON YOUR APPROACH AND TAKEOFF.

IN HER SOPHOMORE YEAR, JACKIE WAS DIAGNOSED AS HAVING ASTHMA, A BREATHING DISORDER. DOCTORS ADVISED HER TO CUT DOWN ON HER EXERCISE, WHICH THEY FELT WAS THE CAUSE OF THE ASTHMA ATTACKS.

YOU SHOULD STOP EXERCISING SO MUCH, JACKIE.

I'LL REST AND TAKE MEDICINE, BUT I'M NOT GOING TO SLOW DOWN NOW!

JACKIE MADE IT ALL THE WAY TO THE WORLD CHAMPIONSHIPS IN HELSINKI, FINLAND, DURING HER JUNIOR YEAR. BUT SHE PULLED A HAMSTRING MUSCLE AND DID NOT COMPLETE THE HEPTATHLON. JACKIE'S BROTHER AL ALSO PULLED A HAMSTRING AND FINISHED EIGHTH IN HIS EVENT, THE TRIPLE JUMP.

I CAN'T BELIEVE THIS HAPPENED.

JACKIE, IT'S JUST NOT OUR TIME YET.

JACKIE COMPETED IN THE 1984 OLYMPIC TRIALS, WHERE THE TOP THREE FINISHERS BECAME MEMBERS OF THE OLYMPIC TEAM. JACKIE NOT ONLY MADE THE TEAM, SHE SET A NEW AMERICAN HEPTATHLON RECORD. SHE WAS ON HER WAY!

SHE'S AMAZING!

THAT'S WHAT I'VE ALWAYS SAID.

She was also tenth on UCLA's all-time assist list. "If Jackie had specialized in basketball, she would have made the Olympic team," Coach Moore said.

Meanwhile, Jackie's friendship with Bob continued to grow. After his success in training Olympic athletes, Bob had been named head coach of the women's track team. "We could talk about absolutely anything," Jackie said. "And whatever acclaim came to me didn't bother him." Her success had bothered some of the men she dated.

Bob was beginning to think of Jackie as more than an athlete. He had been very moved by how gracious Jackie was in handling her defeat at the Olympics.

One night, late in 1984, Bob called up Jackie and asked her to meet him at the beach so they could talk. When she arrived, he said he just wanted to ask her to predict her heptathlon scores for the next NCAA championships. But Jackie knew he had something else on his mind. "Nothing came of it at the time," she said, "but I went home and looked in the mirror and said, 'I think he likes me.'"

Bob and Jackie were spending a lot of time training together. There were no heptathlons scheduled until the summer, so Jackie helped the UCLA team during the 1985 indoor and outdoor seasons by competing in as many events as she could. She ran sprints, hurdles, and relays, did the long jump, and even tried the triple jump.

Jackie was such a fast and powerful athlete, and in such great condition from her heptathlon training, that she was able to succeed at just about any event she tried. She triple-jumped 43'4", which was the best jump by an American woman that year. She ran the 400-meter hurdles in 55.05 seconds, the fourth fastest time by an American woman in history.

At the NCAA outdoor championships in May, on a steamy hot day in Austin, Texas, Jackie qualified for the finals in five different events. All that work wore her down a little, but Jackie still was able to finish second in the 400-meter hurdles and third in the 100-meter hurdles. She was the highest individual scorer at the meet.

During the summer, many top track and field athletes journey to Europe to compete on the international circuit. This time, Jackie went along, too. She wanted to concentrate on her long jumping.

Carol Lewis had retaken the American indoor long-jump record from Jackie with a leap of 21'10 3/4" in Japan, and Jackie was eager to get back into the record book. She felt that she was in great shape and ready to fly. At a meet in Zurich, Switzerland, Jackie did fly, setting a new American outdoor record with a leap of 23'9". "That was as happy as I've ever seen her," said Al, who was also on the trip. Jackie then went to a meet in Cologne, in what was then West Germany, and jumped what would have been a world-record 25 feet. Unfortunately, she just barely fouled on the attempt so it didn't count.

Jackie seemed ready to jump out of any stadium and set records in anything she tried. In August, she returned to the United States to compete at the National Sports Festival, which was being held at Southern University in Baton Rouge, Louisiana. The National Sports Festival is now called the Olympic Festival; it is held in non-Olympic years and is very important to those athletes in the United States who hope to make the next Olympic team.

The other U.S. heptathletes were no match for Jackie. Jackie won the competition in each of the first four events to set a new U.S. first-day best of 3,942 points. She won all three events on the second day, too — the first time she had swept all seven events at a heptathlon.

The only thing that prevented Jackie from setting a new U.S. heptathlon record was her javelin throw. Jackie's best attempt was 147'9", about 10 feet short of the distance she needed in order to collect enough points to challenge Jane Frederick's record of 6,803 points. Jackie finished with 6,718 points, only 85 points short. Still, that score was good enough to set a new NCAA record.

During the summer of 1985, the relationship between Jackie and Bob also reached a new level. After four years as athlete and coach, Jackie and Bob began dating. They decided to keep it secret; they didn't want anyone else on the track team to think Bob was favoring Jackie in her training. But Jackie was sharing a house with teammate Valerie Brisco, so word got out.

"I would tell Valerie that we were dating, but she didn't want to hear it," Jackie recalls. "She would say, 'You're crazy. Bobby? Ugly Bobby?' Valerie would never believe anything I said."

Jackie and Bob got along so well. Bob didn't think he would ever meet a woman who was as fanatical about track and field as he was. "One girlfriend I had told me, 'You put in more time with your athletes than you do with me,'" he said. "I couldn't deny it. What was wrong with me was trying to find a wife outside athletics and trying to convince her that this is a big part of my life and not to get mad because I come home and have four or five athletes with me and ask what's to eat for all of us."

One night that summer, between pitches at a baseball game, Bob turned to Jackie and said, "You know, we get along so well, we might as well get married."

He wasn't down on his knees, but Jackie agreed.

6

Breakthrough!

By the end of the spring of 1985, Jackie had completed her four years of college athletic eligibility and won her third honor as UCLA's All-University Athlete. But she still needed to complete another semester's worth of classes in order to receive her degree from UCLA.

Jackie decided to take off the 1985-86 academic school year and return in the fall of 1986 to complete the missing credits. She had two reasons. One was that she and Bob were planning to get married in January. The other was that 1986 was going to be a big year in track and field. Ted Turner, the communications executive who had started Cable News Network (CNN) along with other television networks, was introducing the first Goodwill Games, to be held that summer in Moscow.

Ted Turner hoped to bring together athletes from the West (the U.S., Great Britain, France, West Germany, Canada, etc.) and athletes from the East (the Soviet Union, East Germany, Cuba, etc.) to compete on the track. Due to the U.S. boycott of the 1980 Olympics and the Soviet boycott of the 1984 Olympics, many of the world's best athletes had never competed against each other in an Olympic-caliber meet. The Goodwill Games would be televised worldwide on one of Mr. Turner's television networks.

Jackie was excited about competing on television in a major new international track meet. She was also eager to make up for her disappointing performance at the 1984 Olympic Games.

But first she had an even more exciting event to take part in: her wedding. Jackie and Bob were married on January 11, 1986. The wedding took place in Saint Luke's Baptist Church, the small church in Long Beach, California, where Bob was associate pastor.

The wedding was like a UCLA track and field event. Al gave Jackie away and also served as wedding photographer. "When they asked, 'Who gives this woman?' I was out in the crowd showing Jeanette Bolden how to work the camera," Al remembers. Jeanette was a member of the U.S. Olympic gold medal 4 x 100 relay team in 1984. "'Agh! I do!' I said, 'and good luck.'"

Jackie and Bob fumbled around so much trying to get wedding rings on each other's fingers that they almost started to laugh. "This," said the preacher, "is going to be a happy marriage."

After the wedding, Jackie and Bob flew to East St. Louis. It was not what most couples would do for their honeymoon, but Jackie wanted to see her father, aunt, and sisters. She also wanted Bob to see where she had grown up.

It was a short honeymoon for the husband and wife because the coach and athlete had work to do. Neither expected the change in their off-the-track relationship to have any effect on their work *on* the track. "I coached her too long before I married her," said Bob. "If she noticed too much change in the tough coach that I am, she'd question that."

Instead of competing for UCLA, Jackie was now running, jumping, and throwing for the World Class Track

Club, an organization that Bob had formed. Many of Bob's track and field athletes who had finished college still wanted to work with him as their coach. Track athletes who finish college often join clubs. The clubs help pay for their training and schedule their appearances at meets. The clubs get money from sponsors. The World Class Track Club was sponsored by International Chemical Industries, a British company, and Adidas, the athletic shoe company.

Adidas also sponsored some of the individual athletes in the club, including Jackie. Jackie had signed an endorsement contract with Adidas. Adidas paid Jackie's travel expenses and gave her a monthly living allowance. They also gave her lots of shoes because Jackie uses a different shoe for each of the heptathlon's seven events. In return, Adidas used Jackie's name and picture to advertise its shoes and clothing.

Jackie was able to add to her income with appearance fees that top stars receive to compete in track meets. With her living needs taken care of, Jackie set her sights on competitive goals for 1986. As she had done for the 1984 Olympics, she started her heptathlon training in the winter and dedicated her training completely to the seven events.

To help improve in the shot put and javelin, Jackie did extra work with UCLA throwing coach Art Venegas.

On April 25, Jackie began her big heptathlon season with the Mount San Antonio College Relays in California. It was a small meet intended to serve as a warm-up for the bigger ones to follow.

Only about a dozen people turned out in the crowd to watch Jackie finish on the second day, and most of them were coaches. But those who stayed not only saw Jackie win, they saw her score a personal high of 6,910 points. That would have been good enough to break Jane Frederick's American record of 6,803. However, during the 200-meter race, the automatic timer had broken, so Jackie's time could not be considered official.

Jackie was disappointed, but she understood what could go wrong at a track meet. She pressed on. Her next stop was overseas to Austria in May for the Goetzis International, a world famous track and field meet. In difficult weather conditions that included rain and cold temperatures, Jackie still was able to score 6,841 and defeat Anke Behmer of East Germany, one of the world's best. What's more, she had finally broken Jane Frederick's American heptathlon record. Now it was time to go after the world mark.

The time and place for that, Jackie and Bob figured, might be the Goodwill Games in Moscow in July. There, Jackie would be challenged by all the best heptathletes in the world, including the East Germans. Plus, the competition would be held, not in front of a small crowd in a small college stadium, but in front of a worldwide television audience.

Jackie took time out from her training schedule to receive another great honor. For the second straight year, the NCAA awarded her the Broderick Cup, as the nation's top collegiate female athlete.

Then in July, Jackie and Bob traveled to Moscow for the Goodwill Games. This was the meet they had both been waiting for.

She got off to a fast start on Sunday, July 7, the first day of the competition. Jackie set an American best in the 100-meter high hurdles with a time of 12.85. She jumped a personal best of 6'2" in the high jump and turned in her best-ever time of 23.0 seconds in the 200 meters. Jackie was leaving her competitors in the dust. She finished that day in first place, with 4,151 points — 50 points better than the first-day world best set by Malgorazata Nowak of Poland in

1985, and 277 points ahead of the two-day world record of 6,946 points set by Sabine Paetz of East Germany in 1984.

The next day, when the other heptathletes hoped that Jackie might run out of gas, she shifted into overdrive. In the long jump, Jackie soared 23 feet, a world record for the heptathlon. Then she went over to the javelin area, and threw the javelin 163'4" — her best throw ever.

That left just the 800 meters. Jackie had the gold medal all wrapped up. But she was after the world record. And Jackie didn't want to break it by just a little bit; she wanted to become the first woman in history to score 7,000 points in the heptathlon. Because no one had ever accomplished it, 7,000 was considered by track experts to be an unreachable mark.

When Jackie came out to run the 800 late that afternoon, the announcer told the crowd that she needed a time of 2:24.64 to break 7,000 points. With the crowd of 25,000 cheering her on, she finished in 2:10.02. Jackie shattered the world record with a total score of 7,148, which was 202 points better than the old record! Sabine Paetz, running behind Jackie, was the first to congratulate her.

As the crowd gave Jackie a standing ovation, the public

address announcer, speaking first in Russian and then in English, could not keep from expressing his enthusiasm.

"It's marvelous," he said. "It's magnificent."

Bob attributed Jackie's success to all the training they had been doing in her weaker events, particularly the shot put and the javelin. But Jackie said it had come because of all the hard work she had been doing over the years. "I feel very blessed today to come here and do this," she told reporters after the final race. "I feel that I've paid my dues. I knew good things would come my way because I have been very humble and patient waiting for this to happen."

Jackie had become the first American woman to hold the world record in a multi-event since Babe Didrikson Zaharias set a record more than 50 years earlier in a triathlon that included the 100-yard dash, high jump, and javelin throw. Jackie had joined one of her childhood idols in the record books.

Many of the sportswriters and television commentators had expected Jackie to break the world record some day, but no one besides Jackie and Bob had thought she would reach 7,000 points. Some skeptics thought it was a freak occurrence. Jackie remembers: "Dwight Stones [the former high jumper, now a TV commentator] said, 'No way you're ever going to do *that* again.'"

But Jackie *knew* she could do it again. In August, Jackie went to Houston, Texas, to compete in the U.S. Olympic Sports Festival (which used to be called the National Sports Festival). It was hot in Houston. The temperature had reached 102 degrees when the heptathlon began and was measured at 126 degrees on the field. During a press conference that Jackie gave after the first day of competition, she had to sit on two bags of ice.

Despite the heat, Jackie performed even better than she had in Moscow. She set heptathlon world bests in the 200 meters (22.85 seconds) and long jump (23'3/4"), and reached personal bests in three other events.

Jackie was inspired to compete in front of an American crowd that included her father, her brother, and her high school coach, Nino Fennoy. "When I saw her come down the stretch [in the 800 meters], I saw the animal come out of her," said Al. "It's the first time I saw the animal come out of her since high school."

Jackie broke her own record by scoring 7,158 points! It had taken her less than a month to prove to the world that

7,000 was no fluke. "To do it again in this short a period of time is truly amazing," said her husband and coach.

When someone asked Jackie what her most memorable moment in sports was, she would point to setting the world record in Houston. "I went to Houston to put on a performance for the American people after setting the world heptathlon record at the Goodwill Games in Moscow," she said.

Jackie also got satisfaction that there were so many people in the stands — a crowd of 16,500 — to watch her compete. "That's a great feeling," she said. "I can remember setting a record one year with about 10 people in the stands.

"I've worked so hard to put the multi-events on the map, as far as Americans are concerned. Now people are finally involved. It's a good feeling to know that people are coming around."

A couple of hours after Jackie had broken her record, she was leaving the empty stadium with Bob when six kids came up to her and asked for her autograph, although they didn't really know who she was.

When Jackie signed the scrap of paper, one of the kids asked, "What event do you do?"

"The heptathlon," Jackie answered.

"What is that?" asked the kid.

Jackie didn't get insulted. She tried to explain. "It's a lot of events. The hurdles, the shot put, the high jump . . . "

"Wow!" said the kid. "You do all of those?"

People were beginning to notice — a lot of people. For her incredible performances in 1986, Jackie was awarded the Jesse Owens Memorial Award as the outstanding track and field athlete. She was also named Women's Athlete of the Year by *Track & Field News* magazine and Sports-woman of the Year by the United States Olympic Commit-tee. In her greatest honor, she became only the eighth woman in 67 years to win the coveted Sullivan Award, given annu-ally by the Amateur Athletics Union to the nation's outstand-ing amateur athlete. She had to beat out U.S. Naval Academy basketball star David Robinson and University of Miami quarterback Vinny Testaverde for that one.

"She beat out a Heisman Trophy winner," remarked her brother, Al, referring to Vinny Testaverde. "That's some-thing I can tell my grandchildren about. She wasn't just the best woman athlete in America. They voted her the best American athlete, period."

7

Jackie and Bob

Even though she was now a world famous athlete, Jackie returned to UCLA in the fall of 1986 to finish her studies. She graduated that December with a degree in history.

Jackie and Bob bought a house in Long Beach, California, and together they made the one-hour drive to the UCLA campus each day. Bob started his second year as the head coach of the UCLA women's track team. Jackie went to the gym or the track to train.

People were surprised at how well they got along. But it wasn't easy being a husband who is also a coach or a wife who is also an athlete. Athletes and coaches sometimes argue over whose way is the right way, and Jackie and Bob were no exception. They were both dedicated to their work, and they would often disagree about Jackie's training.

For example, at one meet, Bob suggested that Jackie enter a 200-meter race, just for the workout. Jackie refused, they argued, and Jackie spent the rest of the meet stomping around under a tree until the meet was over and Bob could drive her home. Sometimes the coach even argues with the husband. That happens when Bob gets torn between his concern that Jackie's too tired to go on and his desire to push her to break a world record.

Bob says Jackie is difficult to coach, and Jackie doesn't argue. "I'm a perfectionist," she says. "I'm always trying to improve on something I've done wrong. So when Bob tells me to take a day off, I'm likely to work out anyway. That's hard on a coach. Here you've got an athlete who should rest, and this athlete wants to do more and more. I just have to realize that when he says rest, I should rest."

But when they arrive home they always try to leave all the track talk outside the front door. "Bobby is a very quiet person at home," says Jackie. "He's to himself a lot. He likes the movies, likes cooking, plus he's a brat at times, he likes to be catered to, just like he caters to us out on the field. So I turn around and do the little things he needs to have done."

Jackie was very happy to find out that Bob loves to cook; she hates to, probably, she says, because of all the cooking she did for her family when she was growing up in East St. Louis.

While Jackie is very friendly and outgoing, Bob tends to be more quiet around strangers. They are very different personalities. Sometimes they even sound like a husband and wife comedy team. Once a reporter asked Bob if Jackie had a personality flaw.

"She's hardheaded," said Bob.

"I am not," responded Jackie.

"See what I mean?" Bob said.

Then everyone started laughing.

During the 1987 season, Bob and Jackie continued to work at pushing Jackie's score in the heptathlon even higher. The number one meet for the year was the world championships, which would be held in Rome in the late summer.

The world championships, like the Olympics, attract the best athletes from all over the world. And, as in the Olympics, the winners of world championships receive gold, silver, and bronze medals. The only real difference is that the Olympics are held every four years while the worlds are held every two years. But to athletes, the worlds are very important, too. In 1987, they were even more important because they would be the last big international meet before the 1988 Olympics, to be held in Seoul, South Korea.

Now that she had broken the world record, topped 7,000 points, and reached 7,158, Jackie set a new goal for the world championships: 7,200 points. For Bob, that meant Jackie would have to improve even more in her three weakest events: the shot put, the javelin, and the 800-meter run.

"Of course, goal number one is to be prepared to win the worlds in Rome in September and the Olympics in Seoul," Bob said. "For that, the 800 is the key. If she's prepared in the 800, she'd be double ready for the other events."

Bob wanted Jackie to be able to run a 2:03. Jackie's goal was 2:05. "It's within the realm of possibility," she said, "and it would make me hard to beat."

Besides training for her weaker events, Jackie also wanted to stay sharp in her stronger ones. So during the winter months, she competed in the hurdles and the long jump against the world's best in those events.

Jackie participated in a series of indoor races known as the Mobil Indoor Track and Field Grand Prix, in which competitors receive points based on their performances. These scores count toward an overall indoor champion title, one for men and one for women, at season's end. Jackie won enough points to capture the women's title. The highlight of Jackie's indoor season came at the Vitalis/U.S Olympic Invitational meet at the Meadowlands in East Rutherford, New Jersey. Jackie won the long jump with a leap of 21'10" and the 55-meter hurdles in 7.45 seconds, both meet records. She was named the meet's outstanding athlete.

In April, Jackie moved her work outdoors. She was eager to compete in the hurdles and long jump on the outdoor circuit, but Bob insisted she spend her time working on the javelin, the shot put, and the 800 meters on the practice field. This caused some conflict.

It wasn't until the end of May that Bob let Jackie enter a competition again, in the Pepsi Invitational at UCLA. Jackie could hardly wait.

Free to run and jump, Jackie went out and set meet records in the long jump (22'7") and 100-meter hurdles

(12.6 seconds). Her 100-meter hurdle time would have broken the American record of 12.79, but the electronic timer had broken, and Jackie's race was hand-timed, which doesn't count toward a world record.

Jackie was ready for a bigger challenge. She finally got the chance to put together all the skills she had been practicing at the national outdoor championships in San Jose, California, in June. Jackie was trying to earn a spot in the heptathlon and the long jump on the U.S. team that would go to the world championships in Rome. But she was also shooting for another world record. "I figure it's all or nothing," Bob said. "You might say that's stupid, but with an athlete like Jackie, nine times out of ten it works."

And Jackie almost did it again. After the first day's competition, she was only 15 points behind her world record pace. Then she long-jumped 23'9 1/2". That jump was the longest jump ever by an American woman in a heptathlon, a half-inch longer than Jackie's U.S. heptathlon best, but it couldn't count as a record. The rules of the International Amateur Athletics Federation, the world governing body of track and field, state that athletes cannot be helped by the wind when it comes to setting records. Any wind measuring greater than 4.4 miles per hour is considered too strong, and during Jackie's jump the wind was measured at 5.0 mph. Still, the jump put Jackie 64 points ahead of her heptathlon record pace.

But the record quest died in the javelin. Jackie's first two throws landed outside the legal area and were called fouls. If she didn't throw safely on her third and final throw, she would get no points for the event and risk losing her spot as one of the top three finishers, who would go to Rome. Playing it safe, Jackie threw for only 130', well below her personal best. Still, after the 800 meters, she finished with 6,979 points, not a record, but still the third highest point total of all time.

Jackie was disappointed after the javelin, but Bob tried to put it in perspective for her. "You have to realize," he told her, "you're chasing your own goals. How can you get down on yourself because you're not up to your own standards." Then he said to reporters: "The only person who can beat her is Jackie Joyner-Kersee."

Jackie finished the week by winning the long jump with a leap of 23'4 1/2", the longest legal jump all year by a woman in the United States.

Then it was back to the practice field. Once again, Jackie had been tripped up by the javelin, and she had a lot of homework to do. "Jackie has difficulty listening until something goes wrong," Bob said. "Now her ears will open a little bit, and practices will go better."

Jackie would have no other heptathlons until the world championships, but there was one other meet in which she wanted to compete. In August, she and Bob traveled to Indianapolis for the Pan Am Games so Jackie could compete in the long jump.

Bob had wanted Jackie to skip the Pan Am Games. Most of the other top athletes were doing that because the world championships were only two weeks away. Instead, Bob wanted Jackie to go to Europe, compete in some smaller meets, and rest. But Jackie insisted.

The Pan Am Games turned out to be well worth the trip. Soon after Bob and Jackie arrived in Indianapolis, a fan approached Jackie and asked her to autograph her picture in a magazine. Next to Jackie's picture was one of East German jumper Heike Drechsler in mid-flight. Heike held the world record in the long jump with a leap of 24'5 1/2".

The photograph showed Heike's legs fully extended —

a position Bob had been trying to get Jackie to try on *her* jumps. Jackie filed that photograph away in her mind. And a few days later, as the long-jump competition moved to its deciding jumps, Jackie sprinted down the runway at top speed on her sixth jump, exploded off the takeoff board, and sailed through the air as if she would never come down. She extended both legs and landed 24'5 1/2" away, tying Heike's world record. She had become the only American woman ever to hold a world record in a multi-event and a single event at the same time!

Jackie was thrilled; being best in the world in the long jump had been a lifelong dream. But Bob was overcome with emotion. He dropped to his knees, crying. Even though he was surrounded immediately by reporters, he couldn't stop.

"I'm so emotional because we were so close to not coming here," he said. "I have to ask myself: Am I so overprotective that I could have kept her from this?"

After they had finished hugging, Jackie turned to Bob with a question: "So now I can long-jump, huh?"

Then it was time for the big event of the year: the world championships. At the end of August, Jackie and Bob journeyed to Rome, Italy, with the rest of the United States team.

The weather in Rome was hot and humid, and the heptathlon schedule was long: The first day started with the 100 meters at 9:30 a.m. and ended with the 200 meters at 7 p.m.

Jackie started out strongly, reaching career bests in the high jump (6'2 3/4") and the shot put (52'6"), and posting a first day total of 4,256 points. It was the highest first-day total in history, 105 points better than Jackie's previous best.

But on the second day, Jackie once again had a disappointing javelin throw (149'10"). By the time the 800-meter run came around, she was still in first place and ahead of her record pace by 60 points. But Jackie had begun to feel the heat. She was suffering from a bad headache and from dehydration.

Jackie needed a 2:14 to break the record and a 2:11 to top 7,200 points. She had run faster many times previously. But just before the race was to begin, she suddenly felt tight and dizzy. "I drank some water and hoped not to die," she said later. Jackie could do no better than 2:16.29 and missed her world record by 30 points.

Still, Jackie's score was 7,128 points, third best in history, and well ahead of second-place finisher Larisa Nikitina of the Soviet Union who had 6,564, and Jane

Frederick of the United States who had 6,502.

After the race, Jackie was so exhausted that she had to sit down to keep from falling down. "This is one of the first times I've ever fallen short of my goals," she told reporters. "But I'm pleased to win the world championship. . . . When you think too much about breaking the record, you end up missing first place."

The long-jump competition, held a few days later, received a lot of hype from the media. Jackie was finally going to jump head-to-head with Heike Drechsler, with whom she now shared the world record.

When their confrontation began, Jackie took the early lead with a jump of 23'4 1/2". Then, on her third jump, Jackie soared off to a greater height that carried her nearly a foot farther — 24'1 3/4".

Heike, however, was not able to perform at her best. She had been hiding a painful knee injury. She gave it her best, but could only reach 23'4 3/4". The pain was so great, she had to pass on her last two jumps, and concede the gold medal to Jackie.

Jackie was sorry that Heike had been hurt, but she had been injured enough herself to know that it is part of sports.

Jackie wasn't going to let that diminish her victory. The two great long jumpers clearly respected each other. After the competition, they embraced and Heike was genuinely happy for Jackie.

There was also news from another part of the Joyner family present at the world championships. Al had become engaged to marry Florence Griffith. Florence was a team-mate of Jackie's on the UCLA women's track team. She had continued to work with Bob after she finished school, which is how she and Al met. Jackie was very happy for her brother.

Florence was the silver medalist in the 200-meter dash at the 1984 Olympic Games. But she was becoming better known for the way she loved to dress up for her races. At the Olympics, she painted her long fingernails different colors, including red, white, and blue for the final. At the 1987 world championships, Florence ran one of her prelim-inary races in a hooded body suit that was covered with stars and stripes.

Florence won the silver medal in the 200 meters at the world championships and a gold medal as a member of the women's 4 x 100 meter relay team. She gave the gold medal to Al to let the world know they were engaged.

After celebrating the engagement and all the medals, Jackie and Bob returned to Los Angeles and went back to work. Jackie took a part-time position as an assistant coach with the UCLA women's basketball team. It wasn't as if she didn't have enough things to do. She just wanted to stay involved with her old team and help Coach Billie Moore.

"She thoroughly enjoys everything she's doing," says Coach Moore about Jackie. "She makes everything feel special. That's her natural way. She could be carrying the heaviest burden in the world and she'd still be smiling."

The rest of the year was filled with parties and banquets. In October, Jackie and Bob attended the wedding of Al and Florence. Jackie herself was honored with three more awards. She won the Jesse Owens Memorial Award as the nation's outstanding track and field athlete, *Track and Field News*'s Women's Athlete of the Year award, and the USOC's Sportswoman of the Year title for the second consecutive year.

But Jackie would not let herself get a swelled head over her success. "If you didn't know her," said her friend Greg Foster, the world high hurdles champion, "you'd never guess she's the greatest female athlete in the world."

8

A Golden Year

By the end of 1987, Jackie was feeling worn out. All the traveling around had left her mentally tired. And all the running and jumping and throwing had resulted in minor, but nagging, injuries and ailments. She was troubled by sore hamstrings, tendinitis in a knee, a sore Achilles' tendon, and headaches.

The winter schedule called for Jackie to participate in just a handful of indoor meets. Because 1988 was an Olympic year, Bob wanted to make sure Jackie was rested and at her best for the Olympic Trials in July and the Summer Games two months after that. Jackie had many, many records and honors, but had yet to win an Olympic gold medal.

And her wish to win an Olympic gold medal was what had gotten Jackie started in track in the first place.

So 1988 became a year of ambitious goals: that Jackie set an indoor world record in the long jump (she already held the outdoor record, with Heike Drechsler, of 24'5 1/2"), another world heptathlon record, and win the gold medals in both the Olympic long jump and the heptathlon. In January, Jackie and Bob made a vow: "Let's dedicate this to two people who aren't here — our mothers. Let's enjoy all this."

Jackie had another goal that would have made her mother proud. "When I left East St. Louis, I wanted to get out and not return until I had made it and then go back to the city and give something back," Jackie says. She wanted to use her success to help kids in disadvantaged areas like East St. Louis find opportunities, much as she had.

Jackie established the Jackie Joyner-Kersee Community Foundation to raise money for sports, cultural, and educational programs for inner-city youngsters. Her first project was to try to raise enough money to open a recreation center similar to the Mary Brown Recreation Center in East St. Louis, where she had first been introduced to organized sports. The recreation center had been closed six years earlier because of lack of money.

Jackie's principal way of raising money was by making appearances and speeches and endorsing products. However, endorsement opportunities had been slow to come in. Track and field, except during Olympic years, is not that popular. What's more, most American corporations have been slow to use black people and any women as spokespersons. So a black woman, even the world's greatest female athlete, faced an uphill battle.

Still, Jackie's plans for the foundation received a big boost when she was hired to be a spokesperson for 7-Up. The company pledged that it would donate $700 to the Foundation every time Jackie broke 7,000 points or long-jumped seven meters. (Seven meters is the equivalent of 22'11 3/4".) They would donate another $7,000 if Jackie broke a world record.

Jackie went right to work earning that money. In February, at the Vitalis/U.S. Olympic Invitational in East Rutherford, New Jersey, she set an American indoor long-jump record with a leap of 23'1/2".

Jackie made the most of her few indoor appearances.

At the Mobil 1 Invitational at Fairfax, Virginia, the day after the Vitalis meet, Jackie set an American indoor record of 7.88 seconds in the 60-meter high hurdles.

But the winter also produced two terrible scares for Bob and Jackie — one on the track and one off of it. In the final meet of the indoor season, the Mobil/U.S.A. Indoor Track and Field Championships, Jackie was competing in the 55-meter hurdles. But right from the starting gun, everything went wrong. She slipped coming out of the starting blocks, then hit the fourth hurdle with her trailing knee and the fifth hurdle with her trailing foot. Finally, she stumbled across the finish line in fifth place, sliding facedown on the track.

The crowd gasped, but fortunately Jackie was not injured. She was even able to joke about it. "If I was playing for the Cardinals," she said of the St. Louis baseball team she had followed as a kid, "I would have scored a run."

Then, while at home one day, Jackie suffered her worst asthma attack yet. Bob was upstairs working in his office when Jackie started coughing and couldn't stop. He rushed her to a nearby hospital, where doctors gave her medicine to relieve the asthma.

Jackie had been troubled by asthma on and off since

1982. But she had been able to control it by taking medication and cutting down on her training schedule. She knew that this kind of an attack was a warning that she needed to take it easier. Still, that was a difficult thing for a perfectionist like Jackie to do, especially as the biggest track meet of her life — the Olympic Games — was approaching.

Although Jackie was already at a level where most athletes would be satisfied to rest, she wanted to improve her technique in each of the seven events. She and Bob studied the tiniest details, looking for ways in which she could improve.

Between practice runs at the long jump, Bob would tell Jackie to concentrate on the next-to-last stride down the runway because that would determine where her takeoff point would be. He would remind her to keep her arms moving during the jump. But mostly he would tell her to relax. "Don't try to be fast," Bob said to Jackie. "Do the things that make you fast."

At the high jump, they sounded like mathematicians discussing geometry. "You want to be completely sagittal before you make the turn to the transverse plane," he said. That means, run straight at the bar before you pivot and leap.

For javelin practice, Jackie worked with Allan Hanckel, who is a specialist in the throwing events. They practiced the running start that javelin throwers use. Jackie had always had trouble with the run-up, which is a series of cross-over steps. But after Allan showed her the correct form, she quickly realized what she was doing wrong.

"Jackie's greatest technical distinction," said Allan, "is that . . . right or wrong, she knows exactly what she's done."

To keep Jackie's skills sharp for the Olympic Trials, Bob had her compete a few times during the Grand Prix outdoor season. Jackie and Gail Devers, who was a senior on the UCLA track team, had fun trading American records in the 100-meter hurdles. In April, Gail ran 12.71 seconds to set the record. In May, Jackie broke it with a time of 12.70 at the Modesto (California) Invitational. A few weeks later, Gail lowered the record to 12.68 seconds and then 12.61 seconds on the same day. A week later, at the Bruce Jenner Classic in California, Jackie matched it. Bob tried to convince Jackie to try out for the Olympic team in the 100-meter hurdles, but Jackie felt she had enough to do already.

As spring turned into summer, Jackie polished up her performances in the other events. At the Michelob

Invitational in San Diego, she won the long jump with a leap of 24'3", 2 1/2" short of her American record. At a meet in Irvine, California, Jackie heaved the shot 55 feet, more than five feet farther than she had heaved it when she had set the heptathlon record. Even Bob was impressed. "As long as we've been together, I suppose I should stop being surprised at what she can do, but she can still amaze me," he said.

Finally July came, and with it the U.S. Olympic Trials in Indianapolis, Indiana. The entire First Family of track and field showed up for the event. Not only were Jackie and Bob there, but Al was trying out for the team in the triple jump and his wife, Florence Griffith Joyner, was trying out for the sprints.

The story of the Olympic Trials turned out to be the performances of the two sisters-in-law, Jackie and Florence.

In the 100-meter dash, Florence not only finished first, she set a new world record of 10.49. In a sport where records are usually broken by a hundredth of a second, Florence broke Evelyn Ashford's mark of 10.76 by almost half a second! A few days later, Florence ran the 200 meters and won the competition in 21.85 seconds, just .14 seconds off the world mark.

The media was buzzing about Florence — not just for her sprint times but because she changed her outfit for each of her races. Instead of the usual shorts and singlet, Florence wore a lime green one-legged body suit one day, and a purple one-legged body suit another. Reporters asked Jackie what she thought of her sister-in-law's stylish appearance.

"I tried a one-legged suit last April, but people laughed and I couldn't keep my mind on my work," Jackie giggled. "That's okay for Flo, but not for me."

Some people wondered if Jackie resented all the attention that Florence had gotten because of her outfits. But Jackie dismissed that as ridiculous. "We're not competitive," she said. "The media try to make it look that way because we're family. I think Florence's sexy appearance was very good for our sport. It attracted many viewers who otherwise might not have watched track and field."

For herself, Jackie was content to dress quietly and let her performance do the shouting. On the first day of the heptathlon competition, despite temperatures as high as 103 degrees, Jackie broke three heptathlon records: the American bests in the 100-meter hurdles, the 200-meter sprint, and the high jump. During a sudden rainstorm, she posted her second-best shot put ever. She set a mark for the first day with 4,367 points.

Then, on Day 2, Jackie long-jumped, threw the javelin only one inch short of her all-time best, then jogged home in the 800 meters. Jackie wound up an amazing 989 points ahead of second-place finisher Cindy Greiner.

Jackie not only won the competition, she demolished her own world record with a score of 7,215 points. It was her fourth time over 7,000 points, something no other woman had yet accomplished once. "Jackie does her thing," Cindy said, "and the rest of us compete for runner-up."

It wasn't as easy as Jackie made it look, though, especially in that heat. At a press conference, trainer Bob Forster had to bring in a rubbing table so Jackie could lie down on bags of ice as she answered questions. As always, Jackie was happy, but not completely satisfied.

"I'm very pleased, but a little disappointed about the shot put and hurdles," she said. "I know I can do better."

Now that Jackie had broken 7,200 points, Bob set 7,300 as the goal for Seoul. But Jackie added: "I don't think 7,300 is my limit."

Jackie wasn't finished in Indianapolis yet. On the final

day of the Trials, she competed in the long jump. Jackie had lost the world outdoor record she shared with Heike Drechsler in June, when Galina Chistyakova of the Soviet Union jumped 24'8 1/4". Jackie was eager to get the record back, and she gave it a major effort at the Trials. Jackie long-jumped 24'5" — just a half-inch shorter than her best jump ever. She won the event and served notice that she was heading for Seoul ready to give Galina and Heike a battle.

Besides Jackie and Florence, Bob had five other athletes who qualified for the U.S. team. But there was one disappointing note for the Joyners and the Kersees in Indianapolis. That came when Al failed to make the team in the triple jump. In a scene much like the one at the 1984 Olympics, when Al won the gold medal and Jackie the silver, Al made his final attempt just as Jackie was finishing her 800-meter run, cheered wildly by the crowd. Later, Jackie cried when she heard the news about her brother. "She cried when I won in L.A.," Al said. "And now she's cried when I lost."

In September, Jackie and family were off to Seoul for the Olympics. Jackie was traveling halfway around the world to the track competition she had spent almost half of her life dreaming about. On the 12 hour flight from the United States to Seoul, Jackie found it hard to sit still with all the excitement. While Bob tried to sleep, she was wide awake, moving around the cabin, chatting with passengers and flight attendants, and signing autographs. "Now that I'm on the plane going to Seoul, I'm really starting to feel it," she said.

Reporters wondered if Jackie, with all of her successes and records, could stay motivated. After all, they asked, what more did she have to prove? "The East Germans and Russians will be in Seoul, and that'll keep me hungry," Jackie said.

Besides, there was that gold medal, which Jackie had been denied by her leg injury at the 1984 Games. That's what she had been training and practicing for these past four years. Jackie hadn't lost a heptathlon since then.

Her time came quickly. The heptathlon was contested on the first two days of the nine-day Olympic track and field competition. The first day she won the 100-meter hurdles, and then twisted her knee in the second event, the high jump. Through sheer determination, she put the shot well and then won the 200-meter race. She finished the first day in first place, and on pace for a world record.

Despite the strained tendon in her knee, Jackie began Day 2 with a record-setting long jump. Unlike the result in 1984, she was not going to be denied the gold medal this time! And when she charged home in the 800 meters, aching knee and all, and not only won the gold medal but set a new world record of 7,291 points, she raised her arms to the sky in a show of triumph and relief. She had come to the end of a long, difficult journey.

As she stood on the victory stand to receive her gold medal, Jackie thought of all the people who had helped her along the way, but most of all she thought of her mother. "I always assumed that she would be with me to see this," Jackie said.

Jackie tried to keep from getting too emotional; her Olympics weren't over yet. Five days later, Jackie competed in the long jump. It was an intense competition. Galina Chistyakova of the Soviet Union, the world record holder, took the lead on the first round with a jump of 23'4". Heike Drechsler of East Germany then moved ahead with a jump of 23'8 1/4". Jackie moved into second place with a jump of 23'6".

That is how it stood after four rounds, when Jackie stepped onto the track for her fifth attempt. She had been a little off on her stride and had fouled on two previous jumps. But this time, as she came thundering down the runway to the cheers of 50,000 spectators at the Olympic Stadium, she hit the takeoff board and soared. Arms moving and legs reaching, she flew through the air. When she came down, Jackie had jumped 24'3 1/2", a new Olympic record. No one would catch her this day. The leap made Jackie the first American woman ever to win the Olympic long jump, and the first American woman to win a field event since 1956.

Seconds later, Bob was on the field, hugging Jackie and laughing. The feat had been accomplished. Jackie had come to Seoul hoping to win her first Olympic gold medal, and now she had two.

And just as at the Trials, the Olympics turned into a family celebration for the Joyners and Kersees. Florence Griffith-Joyner, now called "Flo-Jo" by the media, won gold medals in the 100 meters, 200 meters, and as a member of the 4 x 100 relay team.

Before the family could celebrate, however, Jackie and Flo-Jo became caught in a storm of controversy. The problem began after Ben Johnson, the sprinter from Canada who had set a world record in the 100 meters, was found to have used steroids in his training. Steroids are dangerous drugs that help athletes train harder by changing the hormone balance in their bodies. However, steroids have dangerous side effects: They can cause violent mood swings, damage internal organs, and have been linked to cancer. After the news got out about Ben Johnson, another athlete, Joaquim Cruz of Brazil, accused Jackie and Florence of also using steroids.

"Florence, in 1984, you could see an extremely feminine person, but today she looks more like a man than a woman," Cruz said. "Joyner herself looks like a gorilla. So these people must be doing something which isn't normal to gain all these muscles."

The family vehemently denied that there had been drug use by Jackie and Florence. Sources within the Olympic Committee also confirmed that their drug tests had uncovered no traces of banned substances.

Jackie was insulted by all this talk. "I'm sad and sorry that people are implying that I'm doing something because I've worked hard to get where I am today," said Jackie.

"There are a lot of reasons now why I won't even take a drink. I don't feel like putting anything into my body. It took a long time before I would even take an aspirin."

Joaquim later tried to deny his comments, and the matter eventually died down. What remained was Jackie's triumph as the world's greatest athlete. The testimonials began rolling in.

"She is definitely one of a kind," said her longtime heptathlon rival, Cindy Greiner. "She is one of those phenomenal Michael Jordan athletes. You can't compete against her. She's on another planet. We'll never see her likes again in track."

"I'm waiting for her to start competing in the decathlon," said Dave Johnson, the top U.S. decathlete. "Then we will all have to watch out. That lady is remarkable."

9

Running on Empty

Sportswriters called her Wonder Woman and filled newspaper columns and magazine articles with accounts of her exploits. Everyone, it seemed, wanted to give Jackie an award. In the months following the Olympics, *Essence* magazine honored her for a special achievement by a black woman. *The Sporting News* named her its 1988 Woman of the Year. It was the first time the sports newspaper had named a woman; before that, it had always named a Man of the Year. Jackie narrowly missed winning the Jesse Owens Memorial Award for the third year in a row; instead, it went to Flo-Jo for having won three gold medals in Seoul.

Flo-Jo had decided to retire from track and field because she and Al were going to begin a family. But even though Flo-Jo wasn't running anymore, she was still a big celebrity. Several companies signed her up to endorse their products.

Jackie wasn't jealous of her sister-in-law's fame and fortune. She had endorsement deals of her own. Besides her work for 7-Up and Adidas, Jackie was now a spokesperson for McDonald's. She also did advertising work for The Gap clothing stores, and Primatine Mist, an asthma medicine. Her contracts made sure that a percentage of her earnings went to the Jackie Joyner-Kersee Community Foundation.

Much of Jackie's time was spent on the Foundation, which she ran from a cluttered desk in her Long Beach home. Jackie traveled around the country, speaking to children in schools, hospitals, and churches, usually in disadvantaged urban areas. Some of this was as part of a tour set up by McDonald's. Jackie set up the other visits herself. On one trip home to East St. Louis, Jackie crossed the Mississippi River into St. Louis, Missouri, to talk to 2,000 adoring fans.

Jackie tried to visit everyone who asked. When a group in Belleville, Illinois, wanted her to speak and a scheduling problem arose, Jackie suggested that they hold the event on her birthday because that was the one day she had free. They did, and she came. Another time, she took 100 kids from East St. Louis to New York City to watch the Macy's Thanksgiving Day Parade.

Bob estimated that Jackie spent 216 days on the road in 1989, making appearances, giving speeches, or meeting with people who she thought could help the foundation. It was a tiring routine, but it was beginning to pay off. By that summer, Jackie had raised about $40,000, which she decided to put toward starting her own youth recreation center in East St. Louis.

Jackie remembered the adults who had helped her when she was a kid, and wanted to do something for kids herself. She felt that she had a responsibility as a role model and as a human being. "One's heart should always be geared toward making someone else's life better," she said. "Where I come from, it was a struggle for me. The young people back there don't think there is a way out, and I want them to know that there is a way out. I worked hard to get where I am, and if they want to achieve great things, they need to continue to believe in God, believe in themselves, and continue to work hard. Nothing is going to come too easy

— if you appreciate your struggles, you then go on to higher achievements."

Jackie wanted kids to know that hard work pays off — and not only in sports. "Lots of people have different dreams," she said, "and in order to make your dreams a reality, you have to work hard. It doesn't have to be for athletics. It could be to become a doctor, a lawyer, or in everyday life. But you have to work hard. You have to be willing to make the dream a reality."

Kids were happy to see Jackie everywhere she traveled, and she was glad to see them. But she wasn't used to being a celebrity. "It's still funny to me, having people in airports say, 'Hi, Jackie,'" she said. "Of course, I love to talk about anything you want to talk about, so it's nice. It's like suddenly having millions of close friends."

All of that traveling around and giving speeches could have been a full-time job. But Jackie was still just 27 years old and not ready to retire from competition. All of her appearances, however, left her little time to train.

Bob tried to solve that problem by having Jackie wear a warm-up suit to the airport and work out in the parking lot while they waited for their flight. Once, at San Francisco

International Airport, he lined up five garbage cans for a hurdles drill. Jackie, however, drew the line at that.

What Jackie was training for was not one of her usual events. There were no big international heptathlons scheduled for 1989. So Jackie and Bob had gone looking for a new sport to conquer. They decided on hurdling.

"I enjoy the sport," Jackie explained, "and I want to work toward new goals. I'm not just after Olympic titles and world records. I want to continue to excel."

With that kind of focus, Jackie dominated women's hurdling during the indoor season. In one three-day span, beginning with the Panasonic Millrose Games in New York and finishing with the Mobil 1 Invitational in Fairfax, Virginia, she tied the American record in the 55-meter hurdles (7.37 seconds) and broke the U.S. record in the 60-meter hurdles (7.81). She was undefeated in six straight 55-meter hurdle races until the final meet of the American indoor season — at the Mobil/U.S.A. Indoor Track and Field Championships at Madison Square Garden — where she finished second. Still, Jackie finished the indoor season as the overall points leader on the Mobil Grand Prix tour.

For the outdoor season, Jackie moved up to the 400-

meter hurdles. Because it is a long sprint and also requires hurdling, Bob felt it would be good endurance training for the 800-meter portion of the heptathlon. He also thought that Jackie's strength and speed might enable her to set a world record in the event. The American record, held by Judy Brown King, was 54.23 seconds; Jackie's best time, set in 1975 when she finished second in the NCAA championships, was 55.05.

At the Bruce Jenner Classic in San Jose in May, Jackie tried the 400-meter hurdles for only the second time since 1985. When jumping over the hurdles, Jackie liked to lead with her left leg, meaning it went over first. In the 100-meter hurdles, she was used to the number of strides she needed between hurdles to reach each hurdle with her left leg in front. But the 400-meter hurdles were different. Jackie had not run them enough for her striding to be automatic.

During the race, Jackie kept lengthening and shortening her stride between hurdles. On the second through ninth hurdles, she went over the hurdle with her right foot in front instead of her left. But Jackie was so strong and so fast that she still was able to pull away at the end and win the race in 57.15 seconds. But she had looked so clumsy that when the race was over, she and Bob doubled over with laughter.

A short while later, Jackie tried the 400 again. This time it was at her own track meet: the first Jackie Joyner-Kersee Invitational in Los Angeles. And she did much better. She improved her time to 55.3.

But that was as close as Jackie would come to a world or American record in 1989. By then she was beginning to run out of gas. All of the traveling for track meets and personal appearances had tired her out. In addition, her asthma was bothering her more and more.

If Jackie had not been an athlete, it would have been easier to treat her asthma. But she cannot take some of the more common drugs that doctors prescribe. Those drugs are banned for track and field athletes because they have the side effect of acting as stimulants. Athletes who are caught using medications that have been outlawed by the International Olympic Committee and the International Amateur Athletic Association risk being suspended from competition for from three months to life. Jackie sometimes has to take the drug prednisone to quiet a bad asthma attack, but then she can't compete for two or three weeks; that's how long it takes the drug to leave her body.

Because she was so sick and tired, Jackie needed to take time off to rest and recover. Those were her doctor's orders. At one point, he told her she was on the verge of breaking down from sheer exhaustion.

That fall, Bob and Jackie planned Jackie's 1990 schedule with her condition and appearance schedule in mind. Their strategy called for much lighter competition during the indoor season. Her outdoor training schedule would be targeted at the Goodwill Games, which were to be held in August in Seattle, Washington.

Jackie and Bob hoped this concentration would produce some peak performances. Bob thought Jackie could break 7,300 points in the heptathlon and long-jump a record 24'8 1/2" or 24'9 1/4". "We're going to chase world records until it's time to retire and start working on a couple of Bob Kersees and Jackie Joyner-Kersees in the future," Bob said.

But this time Jackie came up a little short. In June, at the national outdoor championships, Jackie was still not feeling 100 percent; her leg muscles felt sore. She won the long jump, but it was with a leap of only 23'2 3/4".

Next up were the Goodwill Games. Jackie had hoped to shine as she had when she broke the heptathlon world record at the first Goodwill Games back in 1986. And just as she had done then, Jackie won the heptathlon easily. Her score of 6,783 was 547 points better than the second-place finisher, Larisa Nikitina of the Soviet Union, who recently had joined Jackie as only the second woman to score more than 7,000 points. (Larisa's finish was disqualified later when a test showed she had used a banned drug. She was suspended from competition for two years.) But Jackie did not even come close to setting a new world record.

"I don't see that fire in her," Bob said midway through the competition.

The Goodwill Games were the end of Jackie's outdoor season. It turned out that she had suffered a pulled leg muscle during the second day's events. She had to retire from competition for the rest of the year.

Jackie's health problems weren't over yet, though. In November, she suffered another asthma attack. This time, the attack led to pneumonia, a dangerous disease in which the lungs become infected. Jackie had to be hospitalized.

It was beginning to look as if even Wonder Woman might just have to stop.

10

One More Gold Ring

Was Jackie Joyner-Kersee's reign as the world's greatest woman athlete over? Some people thought so.

After her amazing string of consecutive world records in 1986 and 1987 and her two gold medals in 1988, Jackie's performance had fallen off in 1989 and 1990. She hadn't approached her world record in the heptathlon, and she seemed to be coming apart with injuries and illnesses.

To be sure, it had all become much more difficult for Jackie than it had ever been before. Although 30, which she turned in March, 1992, is not old for a track and field athlete (Jane Frederick competed in the heptathlon until she was 36), Jackie had been competing year-round against the toughest competition in the world since she was a teenager.

Reporters now were no longer as interested in asking Jackie which world record she was going to break next. Instead, they wanted to know what she was planning to do after she retired.

Of course, being the kind of person who likes to set goals, Jackie had already begun preparing for her retirement from sports. She was doing the homework necessary to pursue a second career as the host of either a children's television program or a TV show about women's sports.

Jackie's plan was to approach a TV career in the same way that she had made herself great in track and field — by applying her three D's: desire, dedication, and determination. "You have to set goals and then accomplish them," she said. "You can always develop new skills. I got myself a tutor and slowly I'm getting better and better."

Meanwhile, Bob was daydreaming about Jackie trying other track and field events. "If she ever worked on the long jump as hard as she works on the heptathlon, she says she could long-jump 25 feet and I believe her," he said. "If she concentrated on single events, Lord knows what she's capable of doing."

Jackie and Bob even talked about Jackie trying a completely different sport, as did her idol, Babe Didrikson Zaharias, who became a champion golfer later in her athletic career. "Bob is teaching me a little bit about golf," Jackie said. "It looks easy, but it isn't." Bob added that tennis great Arthur Ashe had once told him he'd love to see what Jackie could do on a tennis court with her speed and strength.

Jackie and Bob also want to start a family. But, as Jackie has said, that isn't something you can plan precisely.

But even though Jackie had plenty of plans for her retirement, she had no plans of retiring — not just yet. So in June 1991, just weeks after leaving the hospital in Eugene, Oregon, after an asthma attack, Jackie began her comeback attempt at the Mobil/U.S.A. Outdoor Track and Field Championships, on Randalls Island in New York City.

The national championships are a very important meet. Besides competing for the United States title, the top three finishers in each event make the U.S. team that competes in the world championships. In 1991, the world championships would be held in late August in Tokyo, Japan.

Considering how difficult the past months had been, Jackie's ambitions, for once, were modest. "My goal," she told reporters, "is to put myself on the team in both [the heptathlon and long jump] without injuring myself."

Even Bob spoke softly. He said Jackie was still nine weeks away from an all-out effort. "The key for us," he said, "is to stay healthy, have a good summer, compete through September, take a month off, and then start again in November. We want to redevelop the continuity we had from 1985 through 1988."

Despite her fragile health, Jackie had no problem cruising through the first day's heptathlon events and building up a big lead. On Day 2, she suffered a groin injury. It was hot, she was tired, and she finished last in the 800 meters. Still, Jackie easily won the total competition with 6,878 points, 692 points more than runner-up Cindy Greiner. She also qualified for the team in the long jump.

Bob was delighted that Jackie had been able to do as well as she did. Jackie said she was pleased with where she was; she had met her goals. But she still had another world record in mind — 7,300 points, possibly in Tokyo.

The world championships were an important stepping stone for Jackie. The 1992 Summer Olympics were only a year away, and Jackie wanted to prove to herself and to the world that she was ready.

When the worlds began in Tokyo in late August, Jackie was confident. For the first time that she could remember, the long jump would be held before the heptathlon. That would enable her to get her single-event sport out of the way before beginning the heptathlon. Then she would be able to cut loose, shatter her world record, and regain her status as the world's greatest woman athlete.

When the long jump began, Jackie was off to a flying start, sailing out 24'1/4" on her first attempt to take a big lead over her German rival, Heike Drechsler.

But on Jackie's fourth attempt, something went seriously wrong. Jackie's spike got caught between the takeoff board and the runway, causing her foot to swivel and twisting her right ankle. As she went flying through the air, Jackie windmilled her arms and kicked her legs as she tried to stop herself and land on her left foot. She knew she was hurt.

Bob and Al, who was also in Tokyo, rushed to her side. The pained look on Jackie's face seemed to say that it would be impossible for her to continue. Jackie passed on her fifth jump, but Bob insisted that if the ankle wasn't broken, it be taped so Jackie could jump on her sixth attempt. That was just in case Heike was able to pull off a longer jump. Bob also wanted Jackie to jump so that she would be confident that the ankle would hold up in the heptathlon, which was scheduled to begin the next day.

Heike's best jump, 23'11", had put her right behind Jackie with three more chances to catch or pass her. But Heike failed to improve on her third attempt.

When Jackie's turn came for her sixth jump, she shed her warmups, and to the surprise of the crowd, took her position at the head of the runway. She came running down the ramp, and she jumped.

It wasn't a great jump, but Jackie walked away from it without the ankle collapsing. "Bobby said he thought I was just going to run through the pit," Jackie said. "But I told him, 'You told me to jump; I'm going to jump.'" When Heike failed to improve on her best jump, the gold medal was Jackie's.

There would be little time to rest and celebrate. The heptathlon began early the following morning. Jackie said she felt she could perform at about 90 percent of her ability. That, she said, should be enough to win her the gold medal.

The first event in the heptathlon was the 100-meter

hurdles, and Jackie rose to the challenge. She pulled away from the rest of the field to post the fastest time in the competition, 12.96, and took the early lead in the overall standings. Things were looking as bright for Jackie as the sunny Tokyo sky.

Next was the high jump. Jackie tested the ankle, found it strong enough, then ran up to the bar and cleared 6'3 1/4" to increase her lead. After the third event, the shot put, Jackie had a total of 3,130 points, which put her solidly in first place and on track to break her heptathlon record once again.

It was late in the afternoon, and Jackie paused to accept her gold medal for the long jump to the sound of the "Star Spangled Banner" echoing through Tokyo's Olympic Stadium. Jackie was beaming as she stood on the medals platform; things couldn't have been going any better. Then it was on to the final event of the heptathlon's first day, the 200 meters.

Running in the middle lane in her heat, Jackie easily strode out to an early lead. But then coming around the bend in the track, before the 200 finishes down a straightaway, everything came apart. The weakness in Jackie's twisted right ankle caused her right hamstring muscle to tighten up.

The pain she experienced was horrible.

Jackie's arms and legs were flailing as she tried to stop herself in the middle of a full sprint and still keep her weight off the right leg. Finally, she collapsed to the track in tears as the other runners sped past her. She had to be removed on a stretcher. Jackie was out of the race, and out of the heptathlon. Sabine Braun of Germany would be the new heptathlon champion of the world — for now.

Jackie was disappointed that she had worked all year and had it end like this. But the injury would not threaten her career. She would need three or four weeks of rest and rehabilitation, and then she would be back on the track jogging. The doctors told her it would have no effect on her plans for the future, which means preparing for the 1992 Summer Olympics in Barcelona, Spain. And leave it to Jackie to find a reason for hope amid all that pain.

"I think what happened [in Tokyo] happened for a reason," she said. "I think it will make me much hungrier, much stronger going into Barcelona, understanding that my toughest opponent is myself. I have to continue to work hard and understand that if I want to win the gold medal, I'm going to have to keep my focus."

So, as the days count down to the Summer Games in Spain, Jackie Joyner-Kersee continues to work hard and push herself to greater and greater accomplishments. She does it not because she has to — she already has two gold medals, one silver medal, and a slew of world and American records — but because it is the only way she knows how. There are more gold medals out there to win, and more records to break.

And Jackie has no plans to stop competing even after these Olympics are over. She'll keep training and competing perhaps through the *next* Summer Olympics, which will be held in Atlanta, Georgia, in 1996. "With the 1996 Games being in America," she says, "I think I'd like to end my career in Atlanta."

By then, Jackie might have six gold medals, maybe more if she decides to try more of the single events. And she certainly will have captured her place in sports history — not just as the greatest woman athlete in the world, but as the greatest woman athlete of all time.

"As I always seem to wind up saying," says Bob, the man who knew it first, "She's amazing."

Glossary
Track and Field Terms

Approach: The run by a long jumper or a high jumper to the takeoff point.

Crossbar: A horizontal bar that rests lightly on two vertical supports. High jumpers must clear the crossbar without knocking it off.

Hurdles: The barriers that hurdlers must jump over. Hurdles vary in height and distance apart depending on the level of the competition.

Long Distance: Racing events in which the distance is at least 5,000 meters (3 1/2 miles) or longer.

Middle Distance: Racing events in which the distance is between 400 meters (1/4 mile) to 5,000 meters (3 1/2 miles).

Pit: The highly-padded area in which the high jumper lands, as well as the sandy area in which the long jumper lands.

Relay: A running event composed of teams of four runners each in which each runner runs 1/4 of the total distance of the race. At the end of their portion, runners must pass batons to the next runners.

Runway: The approach to the long jump, usually 100-150 feet in length, in which jumpers run as fast as they can to build up as much speed as possible for the takeoff.

Sprints: Short-distance racing events, such as the 100-

meter and 200-meter dashes and the 100-yard and 220-yard dashes, that are run at full speed.

Starting blocks: Adjustable supports anchored in the track that give sprinters a surface from which to push off.

Takeoff board: The rectangular board positioned at the end of the long-jump and triple-jump runways. It helps the jumper in his or her takeoff. The jumper's foot cannot cross the edge of the board or the jump will not be allowed.